Belief Work

BeliefWork

*What My Traumatic Childhood
Taught Me About Core Beliefs,
the Real Truth, and the Universe*

Krista Rosen

Paradigm Rebel Publications

©2018, 2021 Krista Rosen
All rights reserved.
Second Edition

No part of this book may be reproduced in any manner whatsoever without written permission from the author, except in the case of brief quotations embodied in critical essays, reviews and articles.

Cover Illustration & Cover Design by Robert R. Sanders.
Editing & Book Design by Shawn Aveningo Sanders.
Copy Editing by Mallory Herrmann.

Some names and identifying details have been changed to protect the privacy of individuals. This book is not intended as a substitute for the medical advice of physicians. The reader should regularly consult a physician in matters relating to his/her health and particularly with respect to any symptoms that may require diagnosis or medical attention.

Library of Congress Control Number: 20200944256
ISBN: 978-1-7352540-9-8

Printed by IngramSpark in the United States of America.
Wholesale Distribution by Ingram Content Group.

Published by Paradigm Rebel Publications, 2021
Portland, Oregon
https://www.paradigmrebels.com
krista@paradigmrebels.com

To My Children

Contents

Introduction	9
How to Use This Book	23
Part 1: The False Foundation	27
The Pornographic Photoshoots	31
When Vacation Is a Nudist Camp	39
The Gun Pointed at Me	47
Part 2: Solo Support	53
The Apartment Game After the Divorce	57
Secretly Moving to Florida	65
Gail and Hawaii	73
Part 3: Giving Away My Power	79
When Your Uncle Shows You Porn	83
High School	89
Living with the Parks (Junior Year)	95
Part 4: Regiment of Responsibility	99
My Young Adult Years (1990-1997)	103
Marriage & Family (1997-2011)	107
Healing My Children	111
Part 5: The Patriarchy	115
Trump Is My Dad	119
The Ford/Kavanaugh Chaos	125
Epilogue	131
Resources & Recommended Reading	135
In Appreciation	143
About the Author	145
Praise for *BeliefWork*	147

Introduction

I hear someone calling my name, but I'd rather keep working on my art project. It makes me feel calm, sitting here inside the portable classroom. Someone is tapping my shoulder, and suddenly the voices of my 6th grade classmates and the smell of plaster of Paris make me jump a little in my chair. I turn to see a boy from my class.

"Someone is here to see you."

"Who?"

"I dunno."

I walk toward the door feeling curious and nervous. I open the door just enough to step halfway out onto the stoop of the portable. I lean against the heavy fire door to hold it open as a wallop of heat and sun hit my face. I squint to see that my father is standing on the stoop of the doorway. My father lives in California! This is Florida.

"Let's go," my father says in a firm voice, extending his hand toward my arm.

"Why are you here? Where are we going?" I say in a quiet voice, unsure if I will get hit if I say anything else. My throat feels hot and splintery.

"We're going on a little trip," he says with a nervous laugh and a half smile.

I don't know what is going on and this isn't right. I quickly look back into the busy classroom, searching for my teacher's easy-to-spot dark, thick-framed glasses. He'll know what is happening. I can't see him anywhere! No one is looking my way. I don't know what to do, but I know my father does whatever he wants, and no one stops him. I shudder a little and feel like I may fall down. I'm floating above my body, watching myself as if it were a movie.

My father, Stan, is standing on the stoop of the portable, taking up almost all of the space with his 6'4" frame, wearing gray polyester pants, a black belt, and plaid shirt. He is looking at me, then down the steps, then back at me.

His blank face is weird and wrong, but I need to look at it in order to figure out his mood and what he is up to. I have no clue what is happening! A few seconds go by before my body does what he says, as though on autopilot. I see myself follow Stan down the steps while he holds my arm. He guides me onto the sidewalk then onto the freshly mowed green lawn.

"I parked over there."

"Where are we going? What trip? Does Mom know you're here?" My voice sounds a little stronger now.

Stan grunts and shakes his head.

My father and I walk next to each other, but he is slightly ahead of me, guiding me along by holding my arm. He watches me walk next to him without stopping, so he lets go of my arm.

I feel dizzy and nauseous, as every step feels like I'm in a dream. Classes are in session, so it's quiet and the outdoor corridors are empty. The lawn seems to go on forever. The white buildings and sidewalks fade out as we step onto the shiny hot pavement of the parking lot. Stan points to a tan four-door sedan and opens the back passenger-side door.

"Lie down in the backseat. You're going to have to stay down out of sight."

"Where are we going?"

"To the airport. The Tampa airport. The cops will think I'm going to Orlando. Tampa is a longer drive but more secluded. We'll be harder to find."

Oh my god, my father is kidnapping me! I lie down right away as I know from experience that if I don't, I'll likely get hit or he will just shove me into the backseat anyway. My legs feel so weak right now, something that happens a lot when I'm around my dad. It's the winter of 1977 and I'm 12 now, older and bigger than the last time I saw my dad, which was in the spring, but I still feel so weak around him.

Stan gets into the car and starts driving out of the parking lot of the school. He fiddles with the AM radio, looking for sports like he does when we go on errands. I don't think I am breathing because I can't feel or hear my breath, but I must be. I can't believe Stan is getting away with this! I wonder if the police are going to find us.

I am on my back, looking up at the clear blue sky out of the back window: my only view other than the brown vinyl seat. I recognize the rooftops of the dingy houses and power lines I see when I am riding the school bus. The sky still looks the same as it did the last time that I saw it, when I walked from homeroom to the art portable with my class.

I realize that Stan is talking to me in his usual matter-of-fact way.

"I'm taking you back to California to live with me and Carla. Your mother wouldn't send you and Anne to visit me. She was worried that I wouldn't't send you girls back. Linda was right, I might not have sent you back. Wouldn't sign papers from their lawyer. You know, I bought tickets for you two this summer and your mother didn't put you on the plane. I was there waiting for you at the gate and you didn't show up. I wasted so much money on those tickets!"

"Are you going to get Anne at her school next?"

"I was at Anne's school right before I came to get you. Her school had a letter on file from your mother saying that only she and her parents could pick her up. I figured your school would have a letter too, so I walked around looking for you. I found a student that knew where you were."

My dad is so weird! I wonder if kids were scared of this tall man walking around asking questions about me. So embarrassing! Everyone must be thinking of me and how weird I am and that my dad is a psycho. My school's corridors are outside. That's probably why it was easy for Stan to walk around without the principal's office knowing.

I'm so relieved. Selfish, I know, because I'm leaving my sister with the crazy apartment situation. Wait, I don't have to worry about what my mom will be like after school! I don't have to feel her being mad and pretend that I don't see her pouring vodka into her orange juice glass when she goes into the kitchen. I don't have to worry that she'll want to talk to us and not be able to understand what she's saying. I don't have to worry whether my sister has eaten dinner and had her bath. I don't have to check a lot of times to make sure my sister is in the apartment or safe playing outside.

I don't have to leave the bright blue sky and enter the dark den of our dingy smoky apartment. My school is okay, but I don't belong there. Actually, I can't remember much about my school right now. The way it looks inside my classroom and what the buildings are like is starting to melt away, as if I went there long ago.

I do like Stan's wife, Carla. She doesn't stand up to Stan or anything like that, but she is very nice to me. Stan doesn't give me lusty stares when Carla is around, so that's a good thing for me.

I used to live in Stan and Carla's house before my parents divorced. It's clean and doesn't have a lot of stuff in it, now that we have moved out. I must be getting my old room back which sounds great actually.

I feel super tired right now even though I have no idea what's going on. I feel like I'm supposed to do something, but I don't know what it is.

I wake up and am still in the car. This must really be happening. I pop up in the back seat and take a deep breath, looking at my father as he drives. His blank face looks back at me in the rearview mirror. He seems calm so things must be going as he planned. We are on a deserted two-lane highway. Tall weeds line the road as we pass swampy empty fields and corn fields of different heights.

"Is it okay to sit up now?"

"Yes. We've been driving on this highway for an hour. I've seen only a few cars. I think we're in the clear."

My heart is beating really fast and I picture my sister alone in our bedroom at home. What will happen to her without my being there? I'm responsible for taking care of Anne when our mom is drunk or not home. Before bed at night, I do what I call my "rounds" like they do on the TV show Marcus Welby, M.D. I make sure the coffee maker, oven, and lights are off and the front door is locked. Once Linda left the oven on and it was so scary to come home to a smoky living room from burned food. Once the front door was left wide open. I woke up feeling a breeze and to people talking outside.

Definitely Carla will improve things, but I think I made a huge mistake by going with Stan. My head feels heavy and now I have a giant headache.

I don't want to live with my dad or my mom, ever. I just want to be in this car driving somewhere else. I know I can do better living on my own. I don't think there's anything else I need to know in order to do that. My apartment will be clean, free of dog poop, vodka stains, and cigarettes. My curtains will be open, and the floor will be clear of piles of stuff. I'll put horse posters on every wall! I will play music and have friends over and watch what I want on TV.

"We're stopping for gas."

"Can I sit up?"

"Lie back down before we pull in and stay down while we're there. I think the cops would have caught up to us by now if they were coming, but just in case."

Stan turns the car onto the exit ramp that puts us on an old country road. Empty fields surround us, and the glare of the sun beats down on the hood of the car. Up ahead on the right is an old white gas station with two pumps and a tall corn field behind the building. On the other side of the road is an empty field. There's only one other car around, parked next to the building.

"Okay, lie down."

"Alright."

He pulls in next to the pump. I peak out of the window to see that the gas station building is on my right. I focus my eyes on the dark inside of the gas station, hoping to see the attendant so I can figure out if he seems like he'd help me. There's nobody else around! My brain swells with thoughts.

I could run into the cornfield when he goes inside to pay! This is my moment! I reach for the door handle. I am frozen, my hand gripping the handle. My hand really hurts from squeezing it so hard. My heart is pounding, and I feel close to passing out. My arm feels like molasses and I can't get it to move. Stan walks back out to the car and begins to fill up the car. My moment is gone.

I am an idiot! I put myself into this situation, a dangerous stupid one!

I stay lying down, feeling sleepy again. I rest for a while as Stan drives, until I feel the car slow down and hear the click of the turn signal. I sit up again, not caring if I get in trouble. Stan guides the car off the highway onto the exit marked "Airport." Airplane fumes seep into the car through the partially open windows, reminding me that this whole situation is real. I see the control tower from a distance and wonder if the police will be waiting for us inside the terminal.

Stan pulls out two tickets from an envelope as we walk side-by-side into the airport terminal. He stops, turning to face me.

"I used different names for us when I bought the tickets. Just in case they're looking for us. You're Karen Robinson. I'm Allen Robinson."

"Okay. It's like we're in a spy movie."

"Yes, like the movies."

We walk quietly toward the gate. People are coming and going, walking right by us. We walk right past a security guard and some other airport workers. I look around for anyone that looks like police but don't see anyone.

"Let's get some magazines to read on the plane."

"Neato. I never get magazines!"

We go into a little store right there near the gate. Stan folds a newspaper under his arm and starts to look at the magazine selection. I stand next to him and take a look at my choices. He picks up Time with President Jimmy Carter on the cover and then Sports Illustrated, putting them under his arm too. I recognize Ladies' Home Journal and Better Homes & Gardens from my grandparents' house. But then I see a Tiger Beat with Robby Benson on the cover! I'm so excited! Stan notices that I picked one and takes it from my hands to pay.

As I wait next to him for the cashier, I look down at what I'm wearing. I have a plain light-yellow cotton shirt on, one of my favorites, and a pair of brown paisley polyester pants with white sneakers. I don't have a sweater and feel very uncovered. I might get cold, but I don't have anything else.

We sit down for a short time at the gate reading our magazines. People are going about their day. I watch the stewardess at the entrance of the gate as she walks back and forth around the front desk. Eventually she looks at me and our eyes meet for a second or two. My eyes are serious, and my face is stiff. She is looking at me but not really seeing me as she continues working.

We are in line to board the plane and a different stewardess is taking the tickets. When it's our turn, she looks right at my face and smiles. I halfway smile back and board the plane with Stan.

I look around and wonder if people know what is happening to me. The same stewardess is on the plane with us and walks past our seats. I watch her as she passes us again toward the back of the plane. Another stewardess walks by, smiling and nodding at us and the other passengers.

I get peanuts and a Pepsi from the stewardess. A woman seated across from me lights up a cigarette. I wonder if my mother is also smoking and if she knows that I am gone.

My father and I land in California and begin the two-hour drive to his house. It's dark and quiet, except for the staticky sound of sports on the AM. The area begins to look familiar as we get closer to the house. I wonder if Carla is still awake since it's so late. I hope she is. She'll make everything feel a little better than it is.

As we pull into the garage, I am feeling nervous and not ready to get out of the car. I only have the clothes that I am wearing, not even my purse. It was so dumb of me to leave my purse hanging on the chair in my art class. My journal is in my purse and it's filled with bad things about my family. I am so embarrassed. I know my mother and grandparents will be really hurt by what's in there.

Looking Back

While I was experiencing this traumatic event, I believed that I was responsible for what happened to me that day. I was an idiot for leaving my younger sister in danger. It was my fault that I was suddenly in the custody of my father, a sociopath with a sex addiction. I was powerless against him. Other adults were not a resource to turn to for help.

Why would a smart young girl of 12 believe such disparaging things about herself? She was so brave! The good news is that that girl survived. Not only did she survive, but she flourished.

Today I am okay. Better than okay. Actually, I am happy. I might even go so far as to say I just might be happier than the average person.

I found out that beliefs don't have to be forever. We don't have to be married to these feelings. I learned that beliefs are created only by the thoughts we keep thinking. I didn't realize that I was walking around going about my day under the control of false beliefs about myself and the world. I am now free of many limiting beliefs I created during the first decade of my life. I want to help others feel as great as I do about themselves and experience freedom.

I demonstrated resilience and savviness surviving the kidnapping event, along with the 12 years leading up to it. That first decade was where these subconscious beliefs began to form.

My Weird World

My earliest memories are from when I was around four or five years old. That's when I realized something was off about my family. It was during one of my father's pornographic photo shoots: Stan enjoyed taking nude photos of me, my sister, and my mother. A backdrop and lights were placed on the kitchen table where we had our family meals. Stan would place us on top of a dark cloth that covered the table. It was a family activity.

Many women over the time I knew my father were complicit or participants in the pornographic activities. They allowed my naked body, as well as their own, to be photographed. My aunt, cousin, and an array of women who came and went through our house for wife-swapping and orgies were the backdrop of my childhood.

Our family went to nudist camps for "vacation." There, my younger sister and I were left to care for ourselves and play on our own. I took it upon myself to protect my younger sister from sexual advances of men and boys. I was repeatedly molested. On one occasion, it happened right at the pool in front of checked-out, preoccupied sunbathers, including my mother, aunt, and other family members.

In addition to sexual preoccupations, our home life was designed around the pleasures and entertainment of my father. Sports was always on the TV. Our house was immersed with the odor of epoxy from Stan's hobby of building and flying RC model airplanes. Our living room was filled with balsa wood, large instruction plans, and different tools like screwdrivers and saws. As an extension of Stan, I would be required to sit near him on standby to retrieve anything he may need for his airplane project. This included retrieving a Pepsi or lemonade, or to make him a peanut butter sandwich. He made me sit next to him in empty crop fields for hours in the hot sun while he flew these planes, instead of taking me to a friend's house or somewhere else as promised.

At age seven, I got hit by a car at a stop sign while crossing the street on my bike. My parents were indifferent to this event, even after the remorseful sweet lady that hit me stopped by to tell my parents what had happened. They did not come upstairs to my room to check on me but continued to eat dinner while watching TV.

I witnessed my father's unusual behavior every day. When I was eight, he and my uncle shot my neighbor's dog for barking too much.

By the time I was in junior high, my friends were on to my strange family. They laughed about my dad as they shared reports of seeing him walking around our front yard in his short robe to get the paper or do yard work. He'd even sit around in his robe facing our busy street. I had headaches most days from stress and the fumes of epoxy and other projects (such as painting his car with a spray gun inside our garage).

My mother left the house only to grocery shop or to get to her night shift at the cannery when she worked. She spent most of the day sitting in the dark, chain smoking in the den. She loved watching scary movies and soap operas, disconnected from the comings and goings of the family. Her hair seemed to be always in rollers, and she spent most of the day in her robe or sitting under the crocheted afghan blanket. I was never close to my mother. She wasn't the kind of mom that did stuff with her kids. I don't remember having conversations with her about anything except TV shows we both liked. Most of my memories are of me doing things by myself or with my sister or grandparents.

When I was ten, my mother asked me who I'd want to live with if they divorced. Shocked and caught off guard, I dutifully chose her. Linda moved me and my sister into a dingy apartment across town, leaving Stan in our three-bedroom, two-bath ranch home. Stan enjoyed the boundary game he and Linda played during the initial stages of living apart. He somehow had a key, which he used often to walk in, uninvited or announced, demanding that my mother make him peanut butter sandwiches. I would jump up and offer to make it instead. If she didn't comply, she would end up on the ground by a hit from Stan.

Not able to control the current situation with Stan, my mother secretly moved my sister and I to Florida, near her parents, while he went on a singles Club Med vacation for two weeks. I was excited about the prospect of things calming down, with my grandparents helping Linda cope with life and us kids. They provided more stability but had their limits. I was hoping we'd live with them (they declined), so I asked to go to their house every day. They did not ever come to our new apartment.

When I was 12, Stan responded to this cross-country move by kidnapping me from school. My mother and grandparents did not come out to see me and did not come to the custody hearing. They also threw out every belonging of mine, leaving no trace of me anywhere. The only communication I got was from my grandfather: He sent me religious letters telling me that I was "living with the devil" and that any acts I participated in would doom me to hell. I was pretty freaked out by his implications, adding more fear and stress to what I already knew about my dad. My father was awarded full and permanent custody of me.

All About Surviving

When I was 13, Stan had an affair with his brother's girlfriend, Gail. His brother (my uncle) was married, but that is the norm that I grew up with. Men are never faithful to their wives. Stan divorced Carla for Gail. Gail's husband came by one night, agitated and looking for Stan. He had an intense conversation with Carla outside our front door, which was near my bedroom window. I peeked out through the curtain toward the location of the noise, causing Gail's husband to turn and point his gun right at me.

When I was 14, Stan and I moved into my uncle and aunt's house during the divorce transition. One day, soon after we moved in, my uncle surprised me by walking into my bedroom after school. He told me a story about his visit with a prostitute then turned on a pornographic video.

When I was in high school, I lived with Stan and his girlfriend like roommates, living freely as an adult. During my senior year, my father got a job in Los Angeles. LA was where I was given a second chance. I met a wonderful family that took me under their wing, finding me a counselor to talk to. It was during this time that I fully understood that my childhood was not normal and that many of my beliefs about myself were false. I finally had adults to turn to for support.

Two days after I graduated high school, I moved out of my dad and girlfriend's house. I received financial help and emotional support from two incredible families during this time. That set me up to move out on my own at 18, into an apartment with my best friend.

Figuring Out How to Have a Normal Life

I could write a giant book just about these amazing families, the Parks and the Moores. The Moores helped me eventually attend college to earn a business degree. In college, I was able to make up for the gaps in learning and personal development that had been suspended while my focus was on surviving.

Interestingly, I was able to compartmentalize a lot of my trauma, giving me the ability to have relationships and friends and to do typical things young adults want to do. Putting my issues aside wasn't something I did consciously. I had no idea what was brewing inside me. After working in advertising and the corporate world, my health began to decline. Anxiety, bouts of depression, and chronic fatigue became my new normal.

I wasn't one of those people that dreamed of their wedding or children. I pictured myself happily living out my days with lots of rescue animals, going out with friends and spending holidays with my adoptive family. I had never been around children and was very skeptical of the concepts of love and family. Those things were for normal people, certainly something that I wasn't. I secretly felt I was too damaged and couldn't offer a partner, let alone children, what they deserved. I was very scared of passing down my flawed genes to an innocent child.

I knew I was looking for something but didn't know what it was. I eventually found that I wanted companionship very much and was surprised when a good friend told me he was romantically interested in me. Four years later, I married my soulmate. For the first time in my life, I had a vision of my future, happy with a family. I know part of this was biology kicking in, something I never really believed in until it happened to me.

My first child had numerous health problems, causing me to leave my career behind so I could search for answers to heal him. I dove deep into the world of natural healing. We changed to organic whole foods, nothing processed. I learned how to cook and bake from scratch. I took a gardening class and read everything I could on green living. I built a kitchen garden and cleared our home of all chemicals, synthetics, and pesticides. I became a natural mama! My husband and I benefited greatly from the changes too. We all felt better. Our second child thrived as well.

Beginning Belief Work

I first heard about the profound impact beliefs have on our well-being during an Accunect workshop. Accunect is an energy-balancing technique based on Traditional Chinese Medicine. Founder and instructor Don Ka'imi Pilipovich explained that we all have false beliefs about ourselves and the world. These beliefs aren't actually true or who we really are but are something we create or acquire. They limit us from our full potential.

After learning about them, we turned to our partners to energy check for beliefs. The first one that came up for me was, "People will like me if I am nice." I was shocked and embarrassed! I knew it was true by the way I responded after my partner cleared this belief from my system. I felt a sense of calm and an awareness about myself that I had never felt before. It took me over a week to process this heightened awareness. It blew my mind that humans have beliefs that limit us and cause unwanted emotions and stress. I wanted more of this feeling of freedom. I was hooked.

Next, I discovered the book *You Can Heal Your Life* by Louise Hay. Let me just say that it was overwhelming and anxiety-inducing to read it through the first time. Learning that I have been following subconscious programming my entire life took me a while to wrap my head around.

The Biology of Belief by Bruce Lipton and *Change Your Thoughts—*

Change Your Life by Dr. Wayne Dyer were the next books I read that helped me understand on a mental and a physical level how beliefs impact our well-being. These three books were my foundation to taking my power back.

My studies continue and my research library has grown. I read every day about energy medicine tools, scientific research, and books on the topic of healing from limiting beliefs and chronic health conditions. I always read with a highlighter in my hand and with a pencil to take notes in the margins. I will always be curious and will never be done.

Even the Trump era and #MeToo movement that is now happening as I write this book has awakened even more unprocessed trauma. The similarities between my father and President Donald Trump forced me to love myself more than ever. Trump has also forced me to forgive my parents on a deep level that I didn't know existed. This forgiveness has given me even more freedom to receive love and to be loving and to become more of the real me.

I want to help you find your own limiting beliefs through my stories. I will show you how I healed from these beliefs so that you, too, can take back your power from the beliefs that separate you from who you are. I am offering you freedom: Freedom from programming that keeps you from feeling the joy, compassion, love, and happiness you were born to feel.

How To Use This Book

This book is designed for you to learn how to work on yourself by associating my stories to your own life. Write down your thoughts, emotions, and memories into a journal or notebook as you read through the book.

The book is organized into five main parts, each correlating to a belief theme. I introduce each theme followed by two or three chapters, each consisting of a personal story, the beliefs that were created, reflections and healing.

As you read each story, notice and record the following:

- ◊ How you are feeling? What emotions come up and where do you feel them in your body?

- ◊ Write down what aspect of a story caused the feelings and what specific emotions you had. An example would be if a story caused you to feel anxious in your stomach area.

- ◊ What thoughts are you having? Does a similar experience suddenly come to mind? Examples could be thoughts such as "I'm not good enough," or "I'm not worthy." Write down any thoughts and experiences that resonate with a story.

- ◊ Memories may pop into your mind as you read. Jot those down no matter how unrelated or unimportant they may appear.

- ◊ Are you experiencing any physical symptoms? Be sure to exercise self-care for strong symptoms such as heart palpitations, weakness, shortness of breath, panicky feelings, or anxiety. Feeling grief, anger, and shedding some tears are all normal and healing to clear out of your body and energy fields. When you are feeling better, go ahead and document those symptoms and their associations to your life.

- ◊ Remember to always work at a pace that's best for you. Trust your intuition.

- ◊ After you've finished the stories, sort your findings by emotions, thoughts and prominent memories. You will see patterns and possibly the Beliefs that correlate.

- ◊ Arrange your findings into two columns on a sheet of paper. The left side is for Unwanted emotions, thoughts, and memories that come up for you while reading the book. The right side is for Wanted. List what you want, what you desire, what emotions you want to feel, what thoughts you want to think, what memories you want to clear. This is a common technique that many Spiritual teachers recommend doing. I still use this technique today.

- ◊ Organize your findings into the following categories: Emotions, Thoughts, Memories & Physical. From this point, consider how you want to move forward with your healing journey. Your path will be unique and perfect just for you.

Please Note:

BeliefWork is my term for the collection of different healing systems I used to heal myself and continue to use in daily life. The Appendix contains a complete listing as well as healing resources.

The content of this book is not intended to be a substitute for professional medical advice, diagnosis, or treatment. Always seek the advice of your physician or other qualified health provider with any questions you may have regarding a medical condition.

~ One ~

Belief Theme:
The False Foundation

1: The False Foundation

The first decade of my life set the foundation of what I thought about myself for a long time. My parents were my world and I trusted them. I looked to them for answers, love, and support. My takeaways from these formative years were many false beliefs about who I was. I created these beliefs based on my experiences shared in this book.

I am now free of many of these beliefs—and others I created or acquired along the way as I became an adult. I didn't fully realize that my childhood was abnormal until I was about 13 and in junior high. I was spending more time out of the house and gaining autonomy as I was able to get to my friends' houses. The way other families worked and related to one another was so wildly different.

Here are the beliefs I created:

- ◊ I am flawed
- ◊ There's something wrong with me
- ◊ I am nothing
- ◊ I am unlovable
- ◊ I am no good
- ◊ I am unworthy
- ◊ I am unimportant

- I am not safe
- I am weak
- I am invisible
- I can't cope with life

The Pornographic Photoshoots

My earliest memories, around age four, when I realized something was off about my family.

"Your dad's setting up a photoshoot in the kitchen. Go and put on this dress," my mother says, handing me my fancy knitted gray dress that I wore only with black patent leather shoes.

"Mom, the dress is too short!" I'm trying to pull more of the dress over my bottom where the backs of my legs meet. I must have grown a lot since I last wore this. I start to tear up a bit as I search into my mother's eyes, hoping to find that she agrees. Anne, my one-year-old sister, is crawling around in between us trying to pull up. My legs are bare and it's snowing outside. My mother's face is empty, and her eyes are far away. My chest feels a little sting inside as I realize she's not going to let me change.

"Okay, let's get you on the table," my father Stan says, picking me up underneath my arms. My sister appears next to me and begins to crawl in between my legs. I'm sitting right on my bottom, my underwear touching the black vinyl tablecloth. My legs are cold and stick to it. Stan is standing at the back of the kitchen behind the tripod and starts taking pictures. I don't like this at all, and I want to leave the room. I don't like how my father's voice sounds right now. It sounds weird. The lights are hot on my face and make my eyes hurt. I shield my eyes after the lights flash. I don't feel good and just want to run into my room and cover myself with the blanket from my bed.

After a short time, my mother scoots a chair over next to the table and sits down, fiddling with her clothes. Her face is stiff and serious. I want her to look at me but instead she looks down at her hands. I notice that she has a nice dress on too. It's short but it covers her bottom. Her hair is puffy on top and spills down above her shoulders to flip up. The smell of the Aqua Net stings my eyes a little.

My father places me on her lap, then my sister. My mother has to hold onto Anne tight as she squirms.

"Okay, look over here!" Stan says as he snaps many pictures while the lights flash. This doesn't last too long because I'm grumpy and Anne is crying and trying to get down.

"Okay, for our next shoot, take off your dresses," Stan says. My mother pulls the dress over my head, making my hair staticky and I laugh. My sister's hair is staticky too. I feel a little happier for just a few moments. But I know what's next. I have to take my underwear off.

"Can I keep my underwear on this time, please?" I say with good manners. My parents look at each other, not saying anything, then back at me. Stan says, "Sure."

"Isn't this fun? It's like a fashion show!" my father says. I really don't like this at all and do my best to pretend that I do. I know my father is saying things to get us to like it. I want to get away from him.

"I'm going to take pictures of Mom in our bedroom now. Why don't you take your sister into the TV room? Watch your sister for a little bit and see what's on TV," Stan says.

"Okay," I say, happy to go into a different room.

• • •

The photoshoots continued for another year or so with me. I got more scared and started crying before the photoshoots, so they stopped asking me. Stan kept taking pornographic photos of women, adding to his collection. Many women over time, including my aunt, my cousin, and friends of my parents, were complicit in and or active participants in these pornographic activities.

I grew up seeing blown-up black and white "artistic" photos—some as large as posters—of me and other women casually out around the house. Stan had his own photography studio set up in one of the bathrooms so that he could freely develop his own film and print it without law enforcement knowing. Every girlfriend and wife he had was photographed this way.

When I was 13, Carla was packing up to move out after the divorce.

She found a huge stash of photos, mostly black in black and white, hidden behind some boxes in the garage. She asked me if I thought my mother would want any of the photos. I shook my head no, unable to form any words. She burned the images of my mother and countless nameless women in the fireplace.

Sexuality Suspended

Although I instinctively knew that this behavior was abnormal and somehow wrong, there was nothing in my environment that confirmed how I felt. I also did not know that my feelings were important, that my feelings were a message for me to listen to. Instead, my barometer was my mom and dad, as children do because parents are their world. I used their feelings instead of my own as my barometer for what was considered safe.

In response, my own sexuality was suspended, shriveled up and closed off as a way to shield myself. My own connection to myself was shut down too. I dreaded the subtle voices and noises I'd hear during photoshoots, even though I didn't quite know what they were. I just knew that I didn't like it and would find ways to avoid hearing them, like covering my head with my pillow or staying outside with my dog. I always felt exposed and uncomfortable from a place inside me.

From my earliest memories, sex was Stan's perseveration and source of enjoyment in life. I can only imagine that when you cannot feel love or empathy, what else can there be but physical experiences and pleasure like sex, food, and entertainment? Emotions and the attachments people had were used as tools for Stan. A way to control and manipulate for entertainment.

Because Stan was turned on by physical stimulus, sex was the focal point of his life and, in turn, for everyone else around him because we complied with his world. I grew up following the ebb and flow of his obsession, dreading his excitement and knowing which situations would stimulate him.

The most innocent, nonsexual situations were turned into a sexual remark. A woman wearing a tank top, a swimsuit, a form-fitting shirt. I knew what he'd say next while watching TV. Every experience, comment, and thought was marked in a sexual way. Nothing was just for fun or for love. Nothing served a purpose other than pleasure. This pleasure was primarily physical, sexual.

The air in the house was always dark and had a low vibration. It always felt weighted and dense from Stan's thoughts and Linda's chain smoking. The thick shag carpet and heavy dark drapes (always drawn) contributed to the ambience of my childhood. My life was absent of elements that would break up the feeling, as if someone vacuumed away any air in the house.

Since I shut down my own feelings, I allowed myself to blend and feel only what others were feeling. I was a sieve that captured the thoughts and feelings around me. At the time, I didn't know that this was why I felt so nervous and anxious all the time. I felt sick and uneasy most of my childhood, not realizing this wasn't normal. I didn't realize I was confusing my own thoughts and feelings with those of others around me.

I was like a fortune teller not knowing that I was reading everyone around me. I had ulcers, chronic headaches, anxiety, and dizziness due to living engulfed in the low-vibration, dark energy.

This was the '60s and early '70s. The time of free love. Three Dog Night's "Joy to the World" was playing on the radio along with disco and Elton John. It was socially acceptable to be racist, homophobic, and misogynistic. Women expected to feel threatened and harmed by men.

As time went by, my beliefs about myself impacted me in all aspects of being around people, even in public. Seeing dads and daughters together stopped me dead in my tracks at a mall or the grocery store. All of my energy and focus would be sucked directly at them, like a homing device on a target. I was a perversion reader! My heart would race as I'd assess the situation, fearing for the safety and well-being of the child.

I'd feel helpless, just like I did when I was little. I'd feel angry that others didn't have the same reaction and judge any mother who allowed a child to be alone with their father or any male. I'd look around to see if anyone else seemed to be thinking or feeling the way I did.

I've encountered many children over the years that were, in fact, not safe. I knew how they felt and would send them a knowing look of support in case our eyes would meet. I could feel a pedophile or any molester or molestee a mile away. My energy resonated with them: We were an energetic match.

I heard stories from classmates on the playground about sexual abuse. We were energetically attracted to one another to be friends. In second grade, a girl from my class was raped by her father every Wednesday, which was bowling night for her mom. I began dreading Wednesdays and Thursday mornings, thinking about my classmate. We girls were a tribe knowing the score, standing in silent support of and with empathy for each other on the playground.

I was a skeptic regarding the motives and intentions of men as early as second grade. I nervously told my teacher that I was moving. We moved every year, so change was normal for me. My teacher was a gentle, kind man—but he was a man. To my surprise, he seemed sad to hear the news. He asked me if I could give him a hug goodbye. This was the first time in my life I recall being asked permission to be touched. I said yes even though it scared me; I didn't know how to decline. I hugged him quickly and felt awkward and humiliated by the act, as I noticed that my small body was hugging him at waist-level, near the dreaded privates. Nothing happened that was inappropriate, but my thoughts and imagination got the best of me.

Because I was so well-trained to think of perverted associations, my mind went right to wondering whether he got any sexual gratification from this hug. I really liked him as a teacher. He thought I was bright and told me how smart I was many times, which bolstered my courage to actually raise my hand a few times in class. Painfully shy, I always sat in the back of the class, the safest distance away from adults.

After the hug, I could only remember that he wanted a hug and probably for perverted reasons. I thought harshly to myself about how stupid I was to believe that he cared for me. My beliefs did not give any genuine feeling a chance.

Safety Is Everything

"I am not safe" was the cornerstone belief that was the hardest to clear. I began to feel safe in my late teens and early 20s. I learned how to trust and receive love from well-meaning adults and created lasting friendships. I was able to give and receive love in romantic relationships with boyfriends. I ultimately learned how to feel safe through these healthy experiences.

I continued to heal by revisiting my childhood through watching my children grow up. I'm always conscious of my sensitivities to men, anything sexual, and whether I am safe around them. I noticed that other moms didn't have the same concerns I did, or to the degree I did, over monitoring our kids' safety. My desire to be as "normal" as possible as a mom has motivated me to look at myself and continue to do BeliefWork and healing in general.

My daughter and my son have had amazing male role models as teachers, coaches, and uncles. It's been wonderful to celebrate the fact that there's good people out in the world that are passionate about supporting children.

I am still wary on occasion of male clients and of my daughter being around her friends' fathers and other males out in the big bad world. My daughter has an excellent guidance system and a wonderful father (my incredible husband), which has created a solid foundation of knowing what feels right and that her body is her own property. My son is also solid in this area, and even as young as ten has stood up to bullies and advocated for peers. I am amazed by their connection to the truth and their bravery.

Raising my children in a healthy environment and eating organic, fresh foods has laid a new foundation for me to heal from. Natural healing solutions for chronic conditions that worked for my children have also worked for me.

Energy medicine helped me learn how to ground myself and to feel safe all the time. I've been participating in BeliefWork since 2012 and I don't intend to stop. I know it is the key to reversing chronic unwanted symptoms. Life continues to evolve and give us surprises and challenges that we can use to learn and grow.

Here Are My New Beliefs:

- ◊ Men are safe.
- ◊ The Universe has my back and brings me supportive, loving males into my life and into the lives of my family and friends.
- ◊ I have amazing discernment over people and situations.
- ◊ It is safe to be present in my body.
- ◊ It is safe to feel sexual.
- ◊ It is my divine right as a human to experience the full potential of my sexuality and femininity.
- ◊ I matter.
- ◊ I am important.
- ◊ My feelings are my friends and they guide me toward healing.

When Vacation Is a Nudist Camp

My parents' idea of a vacation was going to nudist camps during the summer. As a young child, I loved going and couldn't wait to get there. As soon as our simulated-wood-paneled station wagon turned onto the bumpy dirt road to the entrance, my sister and I excitedly took off our clothes. We were about to be unleashed and free!

I loved running around the grove of oak trees that shaded the area from the hot California desert. I could breathe better and felt lighter compared to our dark, smoky house that didn't feel good to be in. Naked people were everywhere, going about their day. Some people had very dark suntans from living outside at the camp for months at a time.

My sister and I liked to play "family" with the other kids that also ran around by themselves. We swam at the pool and got ice cream and sandwiches at the snack stand. At night, we slept in a tent that my dad put up with my mom when we got there. Our car was parked nearby, next to the chain-link fence that surrounded the camp. There were many rows of tents, making it sometimes hard to remember which tent was ours.

Uncle Dan (my dad's brother) and his wife Dora sometimes went with us. Aunt Dora was different than the other adults I knew. She sometimes played card games and did arts and crafts with me and my sister. She talked to me about things I liked and looked into my eyes a lot, which made me feel good. She seemed unhappy with her clothes off but did it anyway.

The happy feelings at the nudist camp didn't last. By age eight, I eventually caught on to the real reason why we went to the nudist camp. There, they could find sexual partners. Even my aunt and uncle would do these things. They'd have sex with my parents, switching partners or "wife swapping."

I knew all about wife swapping because my parents talked about ads in the newspaper and then responded to them with a phone call. I'd sometimes meet the new people that would come over if I was up past my bedtime. They always said hello and were really nice to me.

Every once in while I'd wake up in the morning and they'd still be at my house. It felt weird and embarrassing to see my parents sitting up in bed with the covers around them and a different person next to them.

The following summer, I began to see things I hadn't noticed last year. I noticed that people married to other people were holding hands, kissing, or going into tents together. I could hear them moan and make the sounds of having sex. Sometimes several people would be in a larger tent, all having sex together.

Sometimes my mom or dad would tell us to stay out of the tent area for a while. Sometimes the tent door flap would be locked when I tried to get in to go to sleep or to get something. I'd hear people having sex, so I'd have to find somewhere else to go. The sounds made me feel nauseous and like I was floating around outside my body. The idea of people having sex in our tent was gross, but I would push those thoughts and feelings away. I didn't allow myself to feel anything. Feeling things was pointless.

I still liked going to the nudist camp because it was better than being at home.

The Pool Molester

I'm eight years old, swimming alone (and naked) in the middle of the deep end of the camp pool. Suddenly, I feel a hand quickly touch all around my vagina. I stop swimming, treading water while watching an adult man quickly swim away under the water.

I can't seem to move and I squeeze my eyes shut. *That didn't happen.* Within seconds, he swipes my vagina a second time. I feel jolted awake, as though from a dream. I need to be brave right now. Open my eyes. Open my eyes and look around. You have to do this.

I open my eyes and look around me for the man. My heart is beating really fast and I feel so gross and hurt, like someone stabbed me in my privates and my stomach.

I look around to see if any adult is looking at me, realizing what had happened. No one is looking. People are asleep or lying down in the sun, not looking at the pool. I look to see if my sister, who is also swimming, is okay. She's acting normal and swimming around with some girls her age in the shallow end.

I swim toward the steps, breathing hard and feeling like my heart is going to explode out of my chest. I stand in the water, trying to feel normal again. I feel so icky, weak, and mad.

It's up to me to figure this out. I walk around the camp to see if I can find the person, even though I only saw the back of his head. He had brown hair. I walk through the row of tents, something I don't like to do because there are usually sounds of sex and people are smoking and drinking. My legs are still weak. My stomach and chest feel tight and crampy.

I look around for a while and start to feel a little scared. I want my mom. My mom is probably in our tent and I find here there, folding clothes and organizing the tent. I walk in, breathing hard, and sit next down next to her. I don't know what to say and I'm scared. I hope she will ask me what is wrong. She doesn't say anything to me, just hello. Her eyes seem far away as usual. I wait around for a little bit, but she doesn't notice I'm upset.

I leave the tent looking for something else to do that will take my mind off of the pool. I never told anyone what happened. I was used to men staring at my privates at the nudist camp and at home, including my uncle and my father, but I hadn't heard of people that touch little girls' privates.

I stop swimming at the pool but become my sister's personal bodyguard. I instinctively chose this and told no one, including her, that I was looking out for adults that touch privates.

The Teen Molester

One afternoon later that summer, my sister and I are playing with a small group of children. We know each other because our families socialize, and the parents have group sex.

The oldest boy of the group says, "Hey everyone, follow me. I want to show you something." He is 13 and tall for his age.

"What is it?" I say, echoing a few more voices from the group.

"It's a surprise," he says, turning to me. I look into his face, but his bangs sweep across his eyes. Instantly my stomach feels sick, but I walk with the group anyway, watching my sister walk in front of me with the smaller kids, down the path in between the tents and the pool.

"A surprise, a surprise!" a few of the youngest kids shout.

We're all getting pretty sweaty now that we are away from the shady oak trees. We are past the tent area and are walking onto a paved road. The littler kids are walking slower, their pool towels dragging on the ground behind them.

"Where are we going? What are you going to show us?" I command. "I don't like how far we are from the camp."

The boy turns to me, walking backward while he is talking: "You'll see." The other kids continue to walk and talk to each other.

My heart starts beating faster and I am scared, but I don't know what I'm scared of. I feel like when my dad tells me we are going to do something fun and instead he takes me to the hardware store. He's not my dad, he's just a kid. Sure, he's older and bigger than me but what is he going to do if I stop doing what he wants me to do? There's a group here that can see everything.

I walk faster to get in front of the group and stop directly in front of the boy, stopping him from walking. I have to look up to see his face, but I still can't see his eyes very well.

"Tell me where we're going right now or we're going to back," I say, loud enough for everyone to stop.

He shifts the weight of his body from one foot, then to the other.

He does this a few times, takes and exhales a deep breath. He looks down at me.

I take my sister's hand to turn back.

"I am taking you to this empty house. We're almost there!" His voice is a little squeaky and excited.

"Why?" I say in a strong voice. "How many times do I have to ask the same question?"

"I love you and your sister. I want to be with you," he says in a quiet, shaky voice, sweeping the bangs away from his face. I can now see that his eyes are shiny and weird looking.

I suck in a big breath. I hate him so much! He tricked us! He is disgusting just like everyone else! "There's NO WAY you can love us. You don't know us very well!" I can't understand why he thinks that he loves us!

"I do!" he says in a small, sad voice.

"We are going back. Everyone: follow me. It's not safe here and there's no surprise," I say with pretend authority because I'm scared that they won't come with me.

"Why can't we go? I wanna go with them!" My younger sister is trying pull her hand away from mine, but I hang on. I give Anne a glare that says she better listen to me, and she follows me back to the camp.

Not all of the kids followed us back.

When Your Parents Are Swingers in the '70s

My sister and I were "free range," as they now describe it. Whether we were at a nudist camp or at home, we were not monitored. We figured out when we were hungry or when to come home to go to bed. It was the early '70s, so that was the culture for most families during that time. For my parents, their neglect blended in, as seeing kids alone didn't stand out.

I had never heard the words molest, rape, or sexual assault. I knew that the nudist camp was a secret because it wasn't a good thing. I felt conflicted that I liked to go because it was fun for me (until it wasn't), because I knew about the dark reasons behind why we went.

Sexual pleasure was the main focal point of my parents' activities and our family life. This was my normal, as I didn't know any other way until I got older.

I don't know what happened to the other kids that stayed with the boy going to the abandoned house. I am certain that the script he gave us to convince us to follow him was one that was used on him at one point. It was probably used to get him to the abandoned house by an abuser. Being molested was the way he was taught to connect. He believed it was love. I felt guilty and responsible for years after, until I healed in counseling.

Here are some of the major beliefs that were created from these nudist camp memories:

- ◊ I am a freak.
- ◊ Adults are not a resource for help or support.
- ◊ Threats of being molested is par for the course and part of the fabric of everyday life.
- ◊ Girls are sexual objects.
- ◊ Being a girl means you are never safe.
- ◊ I am responsible for my safety.
- ◊ I am responsible for my sister's safety.
- ◊ I am responsible for the well-being of other children I see in harm's way.
- ◊ Parents are not a source for safety.
- ◊ Adults are to be viewed as a threat until proven otherwise.

- ◊ All activities and events are ultimately for sexual pleasure.

Counseling Is the Beginning of My Healing

At 16, the belief programming was still alive and well in me. Through counseling, I discovered that I was NOT responsible for the nudist camp trauma. It took me several sessions to wrap my head around the fact that none of this was my fault. Deep guilt, regret, and remorse spilled out of me. I felt so light and hopeful.

After I discovered BeliefWork in my 40s, my healing really took off like a rocket.

- ◊ Men are safe.
- ◊ The Universe has my back and brings me supportive, loving males into my life and into the lives of my family and friends.
- ◊ I have amazing discernment over people and situations.
- ◊ It is safe to be present in my body.
- ◊ It is safe to feel sexual.
- ◊ It is my divine right as a human to experience the full potential of my sexuality and femininity.
- ◊ I matter.
- ◊ I am important.
- ◊ My feelings are my friends and guide me toward healing.

The Gun Pointed at Me

I always close the door when I am inside my bedroom. It's the only place where I feel good when I have to be at home. The rest of the house is dark without much furniture or decorations. A few photos of Carla's kids and of Carla and my father's wedding sit on the table behind the couch. My father's model airplane project is sitting on newspaper in the middle of the living room.

I can do whatever I want in my room, which is next to the front door and the kitchen. The phone cord from the kitchen can reach all the way inside my room, even with the door closed! I love talking to my friends at night before bed.

I have a lot of time to wait until I have to appear in the kitchen and set the table for dinner. I feel the shake of the garage door opening, so I know that my stepmom is home from work. She's probably saying "Hello, I'm home!" in her cheery voice, but I can't hear it because I have my new Van Halen record blasting as high as it can go before it starts to sound distorted.

My friends and I talk about our favorite rock bands and songs all the time. I haven't heard this record all the way through many times yet, so until I do, I won't know for sure that "You Really Got Me" is my favorite. The lead singer David Lee Roth is a fox! I love lying on my back on the floor staring up at the stucco ceiling, imagining myself in the front row of their concert. I do a lot of my imagining on the floor of my room. I sometimes stare at my herd of wild horses poster, pretending I am one of the horses, running free and powerful. Cutouts from *Tiger Beat* of cute guys like Robby Benson and Leif Garrett are taped on the back of my door, hiding them from my dad's stupid comments.

I lie on my stomach on the green shag carpet, drawing a copy of the Van Halen symbol from the cover while listening to the album. Sunlight is coming through the sides of my closed curtains, warming my arm. I am feeling a little sleepy. I sometimes watch the sunset while

I sit on my bed, watching as it sets below the corn fields.

I hear a man's voice talking at a level that's louder than normal at the front door walkway. I pop up from the floor to see who is here from my window. We aren't expecting anyone.

I open the curtain flap and see a tall, kind of muscular man quickly turn around to face me. I see part of Carla standing behind him, but I don't see her face. He turns back to face her, then back to me again, but this time he is pointing a gun at me!

I drop to the carpet in front of my window and quickly crawl to my closed door. I block the door with my body in case this crazy guy comes for me.

I feel dizzy and sick but I can't move or breathe. I don't hear any more talking. I feel the front door close with a thud that makes my room shake just a little. It is very quiet except for Van Halen. I quickly leave the door to take the needle off of the record, then return to my spot leaning against my door.

I can't move but know I should go see if Carla is okay. My heart is beating so fast and I can't think very well. I don't know what just happened. Did I almost get shot? I need to get up. I feel so weak, but I try to stand. My legs are very wobbly and my whole body hurts. I try to focus on my breath and finally I am able to see that I am breathing. I didn't help Carla or scream out. I really hope that Carla is okay.

After a bit, I have the guts to come out of my room and look for Carla. I smell La Choy Sweet & Sour Sauce so I know she must be cooking dinner.

Carla is standing over the large frying pan, looking down as she is stirring. She isn't looking up to see me like she usually does. She looks smaller and a little sad.

"Are you okay? Who was that?" I say in my best calm voice. I don't want to make things worse by making a big deal out of something. Pretending that things are okay usually helps her when my dad hits her or her kids or when he says something weird, like the weirdo he is.

"I'm fine," she says, concentrating even more now that she is chopping some celery and carrots to put into the sauce.

"Who was that?" I ask once again, leaning on the counter next to her, looking at her face. She's still staring down at the food. I try to be casual about it so that she doesn't get more nervous or upset.

"The man was Pete, the husband of a woman your dad is having an affair with. He was looking for your dad." She says this quietly, calmer than her normal voice.

"Is he coming back?" I say, imagining him coming back after Stan gets home and shooting all of us.

"I don't really know," she says. I could hardly hear her. I feel so sick and so bad for Carla. I thought she would be stronger and have a better time than my mom, my aunt, and other women that I've known around my dad. I should have yelled at Pete to go away. I should have called the police! Hello, *that's* what you're supposed to do when there's an emergency. I think this was an emergency, even though Carla isn't acting like it was. I want to just run all the way to my friend Lynn's house right now, but I don't want to leave Carla alone. I will be brave this time if he does come back.

My father came home and we all ate dinner together like always. We talked a little bit about the police finding Ted Bundy and about my dad's crappy real estate clients. He always says people have no loyalty. Carla seems like her usual self but has less energy. I, on the other hand, am worried about tonight. I really hope Carla brings up what happened. I keep checking her face to see if there is a change or if she's going to say something. She doesn't say anything and neither do I.

I don't sleep very much that night. I keep replaying the gun scene in my head, sometimes with different endings like the gun going off, blowing a hole into my stomach, splashing hot red blood all over the carpet. I'm dead so my dad forgets to take care of my dog, like how he starved my hamster. My dog is hungry and she can't go potty outside when she needs to. She is sad without me.

Pete comes by a couple more times to talk to Carla. I answer the door once, super embarrassed and surprised when I realize it's HIM. They talk together outside on the front entryway as if I were invisible, which is fine by me. I carefully watch every move and listen as hard as I can from the inside of the front door. One time, I see Pete grab Carla's hand in a romantic way, which is really gross. I can only guess this means things will end with my dad and Carla. Such a bummer. I really thought she was going to be different.

Shutting Down

At 13, this trauma was the icing on the cake. I withdrew further into my imaginary world, where I lived either somewhere else with a perfect family or by myself or with my sister. I drew pictures, read books about dogs and horses, and listened to music in my room. I took my dog on walks or rode my bike around outside if I wasn't at a friend's house or at the horse barn.

Dinner was the only time I spent with Stan or Carla. I had almost given up in a way, not looking to improve my situation, but to just survive. I felt gullible and stupid that I believed any woman could be strong and live with Stan. I felt rejected by Carla, the person that wished things were better for me. She didn't try to ensure my safety from Pete in any way.

I struggled a lot with feeling safe in the places I lived during high school and as a young adult. It was a combination of a lot of things, but it mostly came from the nervousness I felt during the incident with the gun and during the kidnapping. (I dive deep into this particular anxiety trigger and how it affected me as a parent in Chapter 4.) My mind would always assume that someone bad was ringing the doorbell, intending to do harm. I was nervous if I was sleeping on the ground floor of an apartment building. I was hypervigilant when I jogged or when I walked alone, especially at night. I second-guessed my judgement when I met new people.

This traumatic event reinforced these foundational beliefs:

◊ I am unworthy.

◊ I am nothing.

- I am invisible.
- I am responsible.
- Adults don't help or support me.
- I am responsible for my safety.
- I am responsible for the safety of everyone around me.
- I am a coward.
- I am inadequate.
- I am gullible and stupid.
- I read situations incorrectly.

Learning to Trust

Learning how to feel safe and grounded was foundational to my healing. Allowing trusted adult mentors in my life to help and support me gave me the positive experiences to keep doing it. Meaningful friendships were able to develop as well. I learned how to live with people in places where nothing traumatic happened. I consciously tried to stop obsessing over locking everything and checking windows all the time and to stop jumping when I heard benign noises outside, expecting the worst.

I wasn't fully aware that I had always lived ungrounded and in a constant low-level state of stress until I was in my 30s. What I thought of as my relaxed state wasn't really relaxed.

When we are feeling safe in our environment, our bodies don't have to be ready to do anything. Our nervous system can truly relax and enjoy socializing. We can really connect to ourselves and others. When we feel overwhelmed to the point where we feel there is no point in fighting or running away, we conserve what resources we do have to immobilize. Feelings of helplessness and apathy can result in withdrawal and shutdown. Connection to family, friends, and our communities are affected by stress and how we process world events. No wonder many of us feel disconnected and alone. Learn more by referring to Polyvagal Nerve Theory in the appendix.

Through BeliefWork, I was able to notice how I was carrying resentment, judgement, and lots of anger toward the nudist camp people, my parents, and my stepmoms. As I became more and more sensitive as I healed, I could feel these little energy cysts inside my heart chakra and solar plexus chakra. They felt like little sticks in my chest that prevented my breathing. I began to clear those emotions (along with the related beliefs) and practiced replacing those low-vibration emotions with love-centered emotions like compassion and gratitude.

Surprisingly, I was able to actually feel empathy and compassion for the boy that tried to molest me and my sister. I was able to feel how emotionally disturbed the man in the pool had been and was able to forgive him too. My intuition tells me that he has passed away from drug abuse.

Forgiveness doesn't right any wrongdoing. It doesn't change the past. Forgiveness only transmutes the negative, low-vibration "emotional charge" into high-vibration light energy. Forgiveness removes the energy cyst from your body, creating space and removing blocked and stagnant energy. This, in turn, removes toxins and other unwanted physical matter out of the body that was blocked by the stagnant energy. It's like removing a large rock from a stream, allowing the water to move more easily and clearing debris that had been caught by the rock.

~ Two ~

Belief Theme:
Solo Support

2: Solo Support

As a preadolescent girl, I continued to function based on of the foundational programing of what I thought about myself. My parents were still my world and my barometer for what was normal. As I began to spend more time away from them at school, friends' houses, and on my own, I created new beliefs based on my experiences with other adults.

It wasn't all bad. I was profoundly impacted by the couple in our apartment complex who saved us a few times. The Parks were the first family that helped me. They taught me so much about acceptance and generosity, and about how a "normal" family functions.

Here are some of the core beliefs about others and my world that I held at this age:

- ◊ Adults are not safe, not a resource, and not supportive.
- ◊ Parents are not safe or a source of comfort or support.
- ◊ Authority figures like police officers, teachers, and government officials are not a source of support.
- ◊ Others know more than me.
- ◊ The world is not safe.

The Apartment Game After the Divorce

"Who would you want to live with if your dad and I got a divorce?" my mother says to me as I'm watching Sonny & Cher.

"What? Are you actually GETTING a divorce?" The living room is dark, so I can only see the outline of her face from where I am sitting on the recliner, tucked under the afghan.

"Yes, eventually," she says, annoyed. She might be mad at me because of the divorce. I thought it was okay to watch TV, but maybe it's that. I don't really know what I'm saying but I don't want to hurt her feelings. Plus, children always live with their mother.

"Um, I'd live with you." I don't want to get up to go hug her or ask her if she's okay. I can't get myself to budge. Cher just changed into a jumpsuit! When she moves around, it sparkles. Her blue eye shadow is to the max.

"Okay." My mother leaves the room. I don't know where she went. Sonny & Cher are so funny! I'm shaking even though I'm still under this blanket. I look around the room and listen to hear if anyone is near. I don't know what to do next.

I have a feeling that things are going to be better after this.

I should go find my sister Anne. She is four years younger than me and doesn't get what goes on around here. She's playing in her room alone.

"Hey Anne," I say in a warbly voice. "Did you hear that Mom and Dad are getting a divorce?" I clench my stomach in case she cries.

"Yes, Mom told me," she says, in her normal cheery voice. I don't know if she knows what that means.

"Things are going to be better," I think, "And you'll still have me." I wrap my arms around her and give her a hug. I look at her face to see if there's anything wrong, but she is the same.

I feel so weird saying this like I'm her mother or something. I've never felt comfortable hugging or holding hands. Even when other people do it, I feel antsy like I'm going to jump out of my skin. I know I'm not doing enough for her, but I feel kind of sick to my stomach, so I just go to my room.

"Hey Dad, Mom said you guys are getting a divorce. What happened?" It's been a few days and I haven't had a chance to ask him about it. Stan does anything he wants, including having sex with other women. This could NOT have come from my dad. My dad is very direct and honest with questions. My mother, on the other hand, would often evade questions and was mostly checked out.

"You know, I've been married to your mother a long time. I'm just kind of tired of her. I'm also tired of being with someone who's hard of hearing." Stan says this as he's digging through the closet looking for his other shoe. "Your mother is a very smart person."

"Okay." I feel like he punched me in the stomach. I did not expect him to say such a mean thing about my mom. How can he just throw her away like she's nothing? She's a person! A person that lets him do whatever he wants and does everything for him! He's probably tired of me and my sister too.

I don't get why we have to move and Stan can stay in the house. But he's the one that owns it. My dad always gives my mom money each week. He's in charge of everything because he owns everything and makes all the money. I'm nervous about switching schools again. I'm in fifth grade now and new schools are getting old.

Two weeks later, my mother and sister and I move out of our three-bedroom house and into a dingy two-bedroom apartment across town.

Our new apartment is actually kind of fun and I feel a lot better not living with my dad. I like being able to walk around with just underwear on if I want and I like relaxing in our living room.

My sister and I don't visit Stan at our old house. He takes us to dinner or the movies every once in a while. My mother spends a lot of time by herself. I really want her to have friends and be happy. She isn't as angry as she used to be, but she seems tired all the time. She drinks more vodka and orange juice in her room than she used to.

She got a job as a waitress at a nearby restaurant. Every day after school, I play outside with my imagination in the empty field across from our apartment. I pretend to be a caveman digging a new home. My dog is my wolf. I make paths to Egyptian ruins and secret worlds. Sometimes I find bones, cans, and plastic bags.

Then things begin to change. My dad drops by and comes into the apartment with his own key. I get scared every time I hear a noise near the door because it might be him. His visits annoy my mom.

"I'd really appreciate it if you'd tell us you're coming by. I don't like how you just waltz in here like you own the place," my mom says. I know she is going to get hit. She knows she can't talk like that to Stan but she does it anyway! My sister and I look up from the TV to see how my dad is going to take that. I'm scared he's going to hit her so I look down at the carpet, bracing for what will come next. Stan hits her on the shoulder, which makes her fall down right in front of us.

"Get up and make me a peanut butter and jelly sandwich," my dad says to my mom, breathing hard with a weird smile on his face.

"I'll do it!" I say as I jump up and run to the kitchen. My mother gets up quickly and is suddenly behind me.

"No, I better do it," she says in her quiet, annoyed voice, slamming the cabinet shut after she takes out the peanut butter.

"Are you okay?" I say, feeling dumb for not knowing what to do. I should have stopped this from happening. My sister is scared and holding back tears.

"I'm all right," my mother answers. I can tell she's pretty mad. I am afraid to walk out of the kitchen to face my dad, but I don't want to stand around like an idiot annoying my mom.

Stan starts stopping by all the time. It is like a game. He likes annoying my mom when he surprises us.

The Bouncer Neighbor

A really nice couple lives across from us in the apartment building. They don't have kids. It is just the two of them. I can tell that they know that we are stressed out by my dad coming by. They sometimes open their front door when they hear my parents fight.

The husband is a huge man who works as a bouncer, a guy who kicks out bad people from the bar. I figure he's very good at his job because he's huge and scary looking. I've never met anyone like him before. When I first met him, I felt too embarrassed to talk to him. Instead, I'd look at his wife and talk to her whenever we saw them in the hallway. Then I realized that a man like him could be so sweet and nice. It feels different to be around him compared to other men. I actually feel good around him. He is like a real TV father, even though they don't have kids.

Once, they invited us over to listen to music. They have an incredible stereo system that takes up an entire wall. They placed large headphones on my head and played me beautiful songs. They smiled at me and asked me questions about school and what my favorite things are. I can tell they like me and not just because I am a pretty little girl. I just love that about them.

The couple told my mother to change the locks on the apartment. She finally did, and we all waited with excitement for the next time Stan stopped by and tried to come in.

And the day came…

My mother, sister, and I can hear Stan fiddle with the lock.

"Shit," Stan says as he bangs and pushes on the locked front door. "Hey! Open this door right now!"

"You need to leave right now," says our big and scary-looking neighbor in his low, deep voice.

"Fuck you!" Stan says, leaving quickly. We hear his big Cadillac peel away.

After a few minutes, the three of us came out of the apartment cheering and hugging our neighbors, thanking them for protecting us. Stan attempted to stop by a couple more times and was met again by our neighbor. Stan gave up the new game.

When Linda Drove Her Car into a Canal

One day after school, I come home to an empty apartment. I don't know where my mom or Anne is. I have a funny feeling like something is wrong, but I don't know what to do about it. I play outside across the street in the empty field with my dog like I usually do, until I see my dad's car pull up to our apartment building. Oh no, this can't be good.

Stan gets out of the car and walks inside our building. My heart is racing and I feel so nervous about the terrible news I know I am going to get. I trot through the field and cross the street to get to my dad.

"Hi there," Stan says. "I've got some news. Your mother drove her car into a canal."

"Is she okay? Was she drinking?" I ask. *She died! My mother is dead!*

"She's okay, just getting checked out by the doctors," Stan says in his everyday voice. We wait for my mother to get to the apartment in the ambulance.

I walk back and forth on the sidewalk in front of our apartment building, not sure what to do. I look across the street to the field, wishing I could still be there digging up bones. The cops may want to put my mom in jail if she was drinking. If she goes to jail, I don't know what my sister and I will do. Soon I see the lights (but hear no siren) of a paramedic truck pull up to us on the street. They open the back and I see my mom sitting up with a large gray wool blanket wrapped around her.

They help her get out of the truck and she's actually okay to stand on her own. I run up and hug her tight. Her hair is damp and sticky and the blanket smells like an old coat in my grandma's closet.

"Hi," I say in a calm voice, trying to look into her eyes. She is looking around us and seems tired and annoyed. She doesn't answer me but walks past me to talk to Stan, who's talking to a police officer a few feet away. I watch her walk toward our apartment.

I join my dad and the police officer. I really want to know what happened. Luckily, she did not get hurt and was able to swim out of the open car window. I wonder if the police officer knows whether she was drinking and, if she was, what will happen next. I don't dare ask the police officer. I hope my mom doesn't get into trouble.

My dad leaves soon after and so do the police and the paramedics. I walk back into the apartment. My stomach has butterflies and I feel a little dizzy. I don't know what to do if she gets sick or how to tell if she needs help or not. I find her lying in her bed. She looks so small with her head poking out of the covers. The room is dark and smells like old vodka and cigarettes. I look around the room for cups of vodka but don't see any. There are no cigarettes burning in the giant yellow glass ashtray, just old butts that have been put out.

"Your dad is picking up Anne and bringing her here," my mom says in a tired, quiet voice.

"Okay. I'll make us all something to eat for dinner. I'll keep Anne away so you can rest," I say, trying to sound relaxed—like what happened isn't a big deal.

"Can you close my door?" my mother says.

"Sure." Keeping her door closed makes it harder for me to know if she's still breathing or not. Now I have to carefully open the door without making any sound. I check in on her after my sister and I watch *The Brady Bunch*. We watch it like it is any other day.

Regrets and Motives

I regret that I was not a more loving sister, but I understand that my heart was closed at the time. With the help of a good therapist, I was able to see that my sister's care and her trauma weren't my responsibility. It wasn't until I did my BeliefWork that I was able to forgive myself and let go of self-hatred and the guilt over my choices and behavior toward my sister.

I can see how Stan would choose to marry my mother and have children. My take is that he learned how to appear normal by copying what normal people do. Everyone got married back then. My mother might have been easy to date and marry because she, too, had disabilities.

The '70s did not have resources like we do today for domestic abuse and support for children. I imagine if this stuff was happening today, social services would have been called and we would've been placed in foster care or lived in a women's shelter. My parents would have been evaluated, resulting in parenting classes or some type of supervision on our behalf.

My instinct to be out in the field across the street from the apartment was healing and grounding. I listened to it calling to me every opportunity I had to be outside of the home. As an empath and intuitive, I needed it for survival. I am amazed by my younger self and how resourceful and resilient I was.

My ten-year-old self anticipated that the police would see that my mother had problems with her life and my dad. I thought things would really change for the better after this event. When things did not change at all, the event subconsciously taught me that police aren't a resource.

Here are the beliefs I created about others and the world.

- ◊ It is normal and appropriate to be disconnected from my mother.
- ◊ Domestic abuse is tolerated and accepted by everyone.
- ◊ Intervention is rare.
- ◊ People have to take matters into their own hands.
- ◊ Having a boyfriend or husband is pointless.

Lack of Love and a Real Connection

I *thought* that my relationship with my mother was like everyone else's. My mother and grandma didn't appear close or normal either. However, I got to witness the nonverbal communication and love between my grandparents. As an empath, it felt good to be around them when they were together.

I did not witness a healthy mother-daughter relationship until I met the Parks in middle school. My awareness about my different family experience grew. I watched parents love on their kids, and kids turn to their parents for guidance and support. Just being in their home helped me heal. I learned that my family connections were wildly different, and that I was missing things that children usually get. This awareness made me angry at my parents, causing me to disengage even further.

I carried resentment, regret, bitterness, anger, and pure hatred toward my parents for decades. I hated myself, too, by association. I wasn't aware that I had these emotions and unprocessed memories until I realized they were limiting me from giving and receiving love.

Through my healing journey, I created these new beliefs:

- ◊ I am wanted.

- ◊ I am a divine child of God.

- ◊ I am worthy.

- ◊ I matter.

- ◊ *I am important.*

Secretly Moving to Florida

"Guess what, girls?" my mom says, looking very excited about something.

"What?" we shout, both jumping up off the couch. It's exciting to see mom look happy. Her face looks like she has a secret to tell.

"We're moving to Florida to live near Grandma and Grandpa. This week!" I've been hearing Linda talk to her parents on the phone about this. My mom is hard of hearing, so she has to talk really loud on the phone. I didn't want to think about it unless it was true.

"Your dad will be on his trip, so it'll be the perfect time. He won't bother us about it," she says in a firm voice that is new to me.

Stan joined a Club Med for Singles as soon as we moved out after the divorce. He began traveling a lot since he was family-free. He told us that he was going on a Caribbean cruise for two weeks.

So approximately six months after the divorce and of living in the apartment, we are on a plane moving from California to Florida without Stan knowing. So exciting! This is the summer before sixth grade. I am feeling so much better because my grandparents (Ruth and Robert) help my mom and I can relax more when we are with them.

Everything is going to finally be okay! They like to do stuff with my sister and me. My grandma makes my favorite dinner ever: fried chicken. I watch her batter the chicken and place each piece into the giant black frying pan. It's so loud and crackly! I get hungrier and hungrier as I watch them sizzle and the whole kitchen begins to smell like yummy chicken.

I have many happy memories of flying out with my sister to visit them. We fly out once a year without my parents. The stewardess carries my sister onto the plane and buckles her seatbelt. I walk ahead of them carrying my pillow.

Ruth makes us fried chicken and takes us to the library. Robert eats his lunch on a TV tray really far from the TV. I don't know how he can see it. I want to sit next to him but it's too far for me, so I sit closer to it on the floor. Robert knows I like animals, so he takes me on nature walks around the trailer park they live in. We see foxes and different birds, including quail and partridge, through the chain-link fence. There is a forest on the other side where we can sometimes spot other animals.

Ruth is very proud of how much I read and how many books I finish each week. It's a little embarrassing because she tells the neighbors about it when we are out front at their place. It's so weird to get smiles from strangers, but I like it and the trips to the library. Reading is my favorite thing. No matter what is going on, I can read and feel great. I can do it in the car, at the dinner table, and around family at any time.

We left our beds and the couch in the apartment. I think the nice neighbors are going to sell them for us. We each got to bring anything we wanted that would fit in our own suitcase. It was hard to decide which stuffed animals to leave behind, but I told them I loved them and to find another kid to snuggle with. My sister did, too, but she likes dolls more. I was never into dolls.

"Hey Grandma, can we just move in here with you? There's the extra bedroom in the back," I ask once we get to their house after the airplane trip. We are staying with them a few days until our new apartment is ready.

"No. The association doesn't allow children here," my grandma says in her firm voice.

"Well, can we just all move into an apartment together somewhere else?" I'm nervous now, thinking about another yucky apartment situation. I guess it'll be a lot better without my dad. I do feel a lot better about that. He is going to be really mad when he gets home to find that we moved!

"No, sorry we can't move," she says, looking into the kitchen. "I need to start cooking dinner. You girls go outside and play. You've been on a plane all day!"

"Okay." I wipe a few tears off of my cheek and walk outside. I feel a little sting inside my stomach, but swallow that down. I have to think about whether there's anything else I can do to make Florida better.

For a while, I ask every day about moving in together. I ask Grandpa Robert when we are alone. I ask my mom when we are alone too. They both say we can't do it even though I have some pretty good ideas: They could ask the manager to make an exception. They can meet us and see that we are good kids who will be quiet. We won't play outside. None of my ideas sound good to my grandparents like they do to me. I don't get mad at them because I don't want them to stop letting us come over. I am always polite and play quietly when I'm there.

Instead, we move into another dingy two-bedroom apartment on the second floor of an older building. It overlooks a courtyard with a pool. My sister and I love the pool and swim all the time with the other kids that live in the apartment complex. It turns out to be a good place for us to live. We get to go to my grandparents' house for dinner many times during the week. Those days are my favorite.

Linda doesn't want to go to the pool with us or talk to neighbors. I thought she could be friends with some of the other ladies I've seen who are moms too. When she wants us back into the apartment, she stands at the second-floor railing and yells our names really loud. This makes me nervous because if we don't hear her, she gets mad and has to come down to the pool to tell us. Once, I was swimming under water when she yelled so I didn't hear her. She got really mad at me, yelling into my face when I came up for air. She really scared me, making me nervous to go swimming. I stopped going under water so that it wouldn't happen again.

There's an empty lot across from the apartment that has become my favorite place, just like the field across from our old apartment. This lot is like a jungle forest. It's so warm and muggy here compared to the dry heat of California. I spend most of my afternoons walking with my little black poodle along the muddy overgrown dirt road that runs along the middle of the property. I love to look up into the branches, imagining I am on a safari looking for monkeys and big cats. I often sit and read with my back up against one of the old, mature trees or just sit there and daydream.

Even though everything is unfamiliar, living here is a nice break from my parents living together. This doesn't last though because I start meeting new men who come over to date my mom. It's super awkward to see strange men entering the apartment at night after my sister goes to sleep. Even with the music on in her room, I can still hear sounds of them talking or having sex. This makes me feel the same way I felt when my parents were doing stuff in our old house. I can't fall asleep very well anymore. Sometimes it's hard to tell if our front door is opening or if it's a neighbor's.

My sister and I share a room, so I can always look over to her bed to be sure she is still there when I hear a noise. I really liked one of Linda's boyfriends that she found through a disability dating group. She said he was boring, which was totally not true! He was nice and easy to talk to. He'd even ask me about school and a few times he had dinner with us. I try to get her to start dating him again so that I won't have to worry about more strange men coming over.

Linda soon begins dating a neighbor, Earl, a nice man with a thick country accent and shifty eyes. He is a big bullshitter who likes to tell stories that I know are partly made up. He kind of reminds me of my dad, trying to impress us with stories and to seem important. He works for the electric company and wears a hardhat and takes a big lunch in a metal box to work each day just like they do in the movies.

Earl can tell that I don't buy his B.S. I shake my head and laugh to myself and go do something else. I think he likes and respects me because he's stopped trying it on me.

Earl and Linda get married a few months later at a nearby church that my grandparents arranged. They seem happy together and he doesn't seem to be dangerous to me or my sister. In fact, he seems to not be the hitting kind of boyfriend or husband.

I am really bummed out to see that Linda is drinking more and more, even though Earl is another adult in the apartment. I really thought that things would get better, not worse, having Earl live with us. She loses track of time, which is new.

"Mom, why is dinner on the table? It's only 3:00."

"Well, I made it early so you can eat it now," she says very loudly in a slurred voice.

"Well I'm not that hungry yet," I say, confused.

"Be happy that I made it for you!" she screams, walking into her bedroom and slamming the door shut. Shaking, I'm looking at my watch, counting the eight hours until 11:00 p.m. when Earl gets home from work. I feel tears coming, but I can't cry about this now.

From now on I pretend it's nighttime and eat my dinner at 3:30 in the afternoon. I don't want to see her mad. Sometimes dinner is already cooked and sitting on the stove top. Other times it's in the oven. It just depends. The nervous part is when the oven is still on for no reason when I get home. I get butterflies and feel scared opening the oven door. Sometimes a casserole is in there, too burned to eat. When my mom forgets to turn it off, I hear a popping sound come from the oven as it's making heat adjustments and I realize I need to turn it off. If I tell my mom that she left the oven on, she gets mad and goes to her room, slamming the door behind her.

Notes are left for us on the table telling us what's for dinner, chores we need to do, and other stuff like when she's going to work. Sometimes notes mean she's drinking in her room and that she really doesn't want to talk to us. My mom's handwriting is wavy and curly when she is drinking. Sometimes it looks normal, but if you look closely there are little circles instead of dots for i's. Sometimes circles are on letters where you don't need a dot. The harder it is to read, the more drunk she is. I worry that a note is waiting for me when I hop off the bus and start walking to our apartment.

Being the Grownup

I really felt like the grownup in the house. I had headaches and my stomach always felt sick. My mother's changing moods and behaviors caused me chronic anxiety. I was very angry and frustrated by my grandparents not living with us or coming to the apartment. I felt betrayed and lied to when they gave me their fake answers. They knew that I knew they didn't want to live with us, period. This stung and I felt betrayed by people I thought loved us and wanted to help us, which is why we moved to Florida in the first place.

Earl didn't contribute at all except for making me feel safe at night and by being in charge of my mom when he was home. I felt responsible for my sister and myself. I was getting tired of feeling worried all of the time.

Linda's Bigger Impact

My healing really took off after I was contacted by a friend via Facebook in 2014. I had gone to middle school with her while living in that Florida apartment. We talked on the phone for a long time. I was hoping that her voice would trigger memories of her and the time in Florida that would help me heal. Unfortunately, I had completely blocked her out.

She was traumatized by my kidnapping and always wondered what happened to me. She talked to my mom a few times after it happened but then never heard back from her.

To this day, I have no memory of her. This motivated me to meditate over remembering her and more about that year, intending to clear out residual trauma and emotions that are blocking me from healing. I also wanted to remember her and positive things about that time.

I realized that I had made up a better version of my mom in order to deal with reality. I pretended that my mother was more of an innocent party, more of a victim, like my sister and me, of my dad's abuse. I contributed more than his share of responsibility behind my traumas to him.

Realizing that Linda had contributed far more to the false beliefs I created about myself and other people, I connected to the bitterness and resentment that I had buried deep into my subconscious. As a result, a whole new round of healing and forgiveness toward my mother took hold. I was ready because I knew that the healing would benefit my mother as well as my daughter. Healing the mother line had unexpected, exponential benefits.

Gail and Hawaii

When Stan and Gail first got together, they were both married to other people. Since Stan enjoyed traveling, he had booked a vacation to Hawaii for himself, Carla, me, and Carla's sons. After Stan left Carla for Gail, a shy receptionist his brother had been dating, he kept the vacation and instead took Gail and me (as a reluctant and awkward tagalong).

I don't know why Stan chose to bring me with them, as I was totally independent and didn't require any care. Perhaps it was because the ticket was nonrefundable. I was feeling stressed and still processing the newness of Carla moving out and Gail taking her place—and adjusting to Gail's mood swings. I felt guilty about going to Hawaii because of Carla. I do not know why Gail's little girl, Jessica, did not go with us. She must've been with her father or Gail's parents. I began to allow myself to be a little bit excited about the trip and to just enjoy being in a beautiful place. I had never been on a vacation like that before. We had only flown to visit my grandparents in Florida.

On our first night in Honolulu, Gail and I start getting ready to go out to dinner. At 14, I have been looking forward to us girls preparing for a night out like I saw in the movie *Grease*. I like looking more mature. I have fun trying makeup on with my friends. We do each other's faces sometimes when I sleep over at their houses. Gail is much younger than my dad and has great style. I think we'll be closer now. She's been really sweet to me lately. Maybe I'm wrong about this trip. I really hadn't wanted to go with them, so gross and awkward because there's no place for me in their room.

Gail and I are standing at the mirror putting on makeup and curling our hair. She stops, turns to me, and starts yelling.

"You think you're so pretty now, don't you? Look at the faces you're making at yourself in the mirror. You are so conceited and you look ridiculous!" I hear her talking but her words start to fade into the background. I don't know what she is saying and I don't know what to say back. All I know is that I have to run out of this hotel room.

I run out, taking the stairs down to the street. I walk and walk for a long time. I feel so ashamed, thinking I was pretty and then making Gail feel bad. This makes me mad that I can't just relax around her. I just wanted to do makeup and look nice.

I am walking alone in Waikiki but I'm not afraid. I know I probably should be, as I'm getting stared at by men standing outside of bars and restaurants, drinking beer. I spend hours walking around window-shopping and people-watching. It helps me relax. I watch strangers and imagine how they know each other. As the streets get quieter, I start to feel unsafe. It's frustrating and embarrassing to go back to the hotel, but I don't know what else to do.

I knock but no one is inside our room. Stan and Gail must've gone to dinner and are still out, so I sit on the carpet at the door of the hotel room and fall asleep. I was pretty wiped. I hear their voices coming down the hall from the elevator, so I sit up and slowly stand. I feel pretty weak and tired.

"Hi," they both say with forced smiles, pretending that nothing happened. They open the door and I follow them inside but do not respond.

I plop down on the couch to go to sleep, mad but knowing that saying anything isn't going to help. I block out any sounds they make with the couch pillows.

Pain and Betrayal

I was devastated and crushed by her words. My fragile little self was ready to fly and got stomped on before takeoff. Stan intervening wasn't even a thought. I have no idea if he said anything. Gail was the fourth in line after my mother, my grandmother, and Carla to reject me or not stand up for me in just three years. I got the message loud and clear: Never ever trust women. Even the nice ones like Carla or my aunt. They have their own problems that absorb every ounce of their attention for themselves. Being nice is irrelevant when it comes to support.

I also learned that it's risky to feel good about yourself or openly happy in front of others. You can make others feel badly about themselves when you do, reinforcing the need to feel responsible for everyone's happiness (see Chapter 4).

The feedback I got from Gail was mixed. Sometimes she was open and caring to me. Other times, she'd use me as an outlet to her frustrations with her life or with my dad. There wasn't a sure-fire way to tell what you were going to get, even in a scenario that had had a certain outcome repeatedly in the past. This resulted in me not trusting my own judgement. I felt hopeless and just shut down. I couldn't feel joy for years.

In this situation, being alone was my only option according to my environment. Being away from the stressful people or situations felt so much better.

Here's what I learned:

- ◊ People are not trustworthy or reliable.
- ◊ People can turn on you at any time.
- ◊ I am nothing.
- ◊ I am powerless.
- ◊ I can't trust my intuition.
- ◊ It is normal for women to not feel good about themselves.
- ◊ I am expected not to feel good about myself or to like myself.

Becoming Vulnerable and Free

Man, I learned much more from her! I didn't feel good looking in the mirror until I was in college. The amazing experience of taking an African dance class when I was a senior in high school motivated me to take dance classes in college. It was a safe place to experiment with being physically sexual and creative. I could put myself out there and feel like an idiot and no one would put me down like Gail did. Girls gathered around me, supporting me and even cheering me on as I practiced new choreography. These classes brought me more joy and healing than anything had since horses. Through dance, I stumbled upon my inner being. I became reacquainted with myself and with a passion for the endorphin high I got after the intense workouts. I got strong and fit.

Little did I know how movement and expressing myself creatively was saving me. The music of Madonna, Prince, and George Michael fueled and empowered me. Years of unprocessed emotions toward my parents and my dad's wives stored in my sacral chakra had a way out, healing me. This outlet allowed me the opportunity to cultivate "normal" relationships.

Dance classes and music anchored me and became the background in my life, much like horses had in my younger years.

Here are some of the new beliefs I formed:

◊ It is safe to express myself through my body.

◊ Dance is a safe place to feel sexual.

◊ It is safe to feel love for myself.

◊ It is safe to grow up, expand, and try new things.

Healing the energy of my maternal line through personal development work and energy medicine was instrumental. There must be reasons why my grandmother and mother were aloof and distant. I may never know the details, but I knew that my children might struggle with these things, too, if I didn't heal myself.

With energy medicine, one can heal themselves from false beliefs and stagnant emotions. If a child has inherited any of these unwanted beliefs or emotions, they will clear from them as well. This concept was hard for me to wrap my head around, until I noticed a pattern with my healing and clearing symptoms being reflected in my own children. If I cleared some major issues, one of my children might experience symptoms the next day or two if they inherited that belief or emotion from me. Energy testing would confirm this for me.

~ Three ~

Belief Theme:
Giving Away My Power

3: Giving Away My Power

By the time my dad kidnapped me from school, false beliefs about myself and the world were hardwired into my personality. I evaluated myself and future outcomes by applying these beliefs so I could feel safe and increase my chances for survival. Being present in my body got harder and harder to do as time went by. My normal state was to be shut off from my instincts and my inner being. Instead, I continued to give power over my thoughts to my dad, Gail, my uncle, and their friends and families, making them my barometer for what was good. If their needs were met and they were relaxed and happy, then I could be too. The next three stories illustrate how my foundational beliefs affected my relationships and choices.

Here are some of my foundational beliefs:

- ◊ I am powerless.
- ◊ I have no control over my life or my body.
- ◊ I can't express myself.
- ◊ I can't be present.
- ◊ I am a target because I'm pretty and female.
- ◊ I am less than.
- ◊ I am unwanted.

- ◊ Having a weird dad makes me weird too.
- ◊ I am not worthy of friendships.

When Your Uncle Shows You Porn

Living with Uncle Glenn and Aunt Laura during my dad's divorce from Carla is the next best thing to them not getting a divorce at all. They live in my neighborhood, so I don't have to change schools or my routine with my friends. I really worry about when I will have to live with my dad by myself, so for now I can relax because Aunt Laura and Uncle Glenn are in the house with us.

I'm reading a Nancy Drew book on the bed in their guest room, my room while we stay here. The bedspread is slippery and scratchy, printed with tiny blue and green flowers. I'm sprawled out, relaxing after school like usual. Everyone is at work. I feel the vibration of the garage door opening and wonder who is home. Could be Uncle Glenn because he's a real estate agent with different work hours.

The door to my room suddenly opens and my uncle walks in looking excited and frustrated. This scares the crap out of me. I bolt upright, my book flying off of my lap and onto the floor.

"You'll never guess what happened to me today!" my uncle announces. His hair is a little messy and his suit is rumpled. He starts pacing around the room and stops in front of the window, looking out onto the lawn in the backyard. One of his clients must've dropped him or maybe he sold a house!

"What? Are you okay? You look upset!" I say, suddenly feeling anxious and a little sick to my stomach. My uncle is weird like my dad, but you can't tell right away. He is not acting normally right now and he's giving me a strange look. His eyes are burning into my body.

"I got ripped off by a hooker! She gave me oral sex, which is what I paid for. Afterwards, I gave HER oral sex as a favor. She should be grateful that I'd even consider doing that to her after where's she's been. And after it's over, she charges me for the oral sex I gave to HER. Ridiculous!"

"Oh, sorry," I say, stunned as he goes on and on about his bad day at the office and now this. I nod at the right times, pretending that I understand what he's talking about and that this is a normal conversation. I know I must stay focused on what he's saying even though I'm feeling dizzy and weak. It's so hard to think right now. My stomach tightens, bracing for whatever is coming my way next. I am glad I still have on my school clothes. The window is right there. It's the same kind of window I have at my house, easy to fling open and hit the screen off to climb out.

"Have you ever seen sex on video?"

"Uh-uh," shaking my head, looking down to pick at fibers sticking out of the bedspread.

"You should watch this one movie. It's really good." My uncle is reaching for a beta tape and pops it into the machine I hadn't noticed was next to the TV. I sit motionless, watching him watch the screen until the title "Pizza Boy" comes on the screen.

"Okay, it's on now. Here you go!" my uncle says, leaving the room as quickly as he entered it. I am shocked by what I see. I keep watching for a few minutes, then get up to turn it off and lock the bedroom door.

The next day I ask my dad if I can move back in with Carla. I just blurt it out. A made-up excuse flows out of my mouth like someone else is talking instead.

"Dad, this house is too cramped for all of us being here and sharing a bathroom. Our house is empty, including my own room. I don't think Carla would mind if I lived with her until she moves out."

"She's probably fine with that," Stan says in his neutral voice, not looking up from reading the papers he brought home in his briefcase.

"I'll give her a call and ask her today," I say, a little annoyed that Stan didn't think of this himself. Why move me out when I could've stayed with Carla the whole time? Carla isn't mad at me over their divorce. I know because she told me that she genuinely cared for me.

I move back home right away. I can tell Carla is glad to have me there with her.

Once Carla does move out, Stan moves Gail, his new girlfriend, in without skipping a beat. Gail was originally Uncle Glenn's girlfriend. They worked in the same office. Glenn said he "passed her along" to Stan. Gail and her toddler Jessica move right into our house the next week. I never saw her husband Pete again, but I know Jessica would sometimes see him if Gail made a stink about it.

Here are the beliefs reinforced by this incident:

- ◊ I am responsible for the behavior of others.
- ◊ No one will help me.
- ◊ I am not safe.
- ◊ Women are here to sexually gratify and serve men.
- ◊ Women and children are dispensable.
- ◊ I do not belong.

Saving Myself from Further Harm

Glenn and Stan were close in age and had very similar personalities. It was like they were allies, on the same page with their obsessions, perversions, and ways of thinking. They talked about taking advantage of people and situations like they were little kids winning a playground game.

I didn't know what oral sex or porn was. Video porn was relatively new to the mainstream scene in 1978. Up to this point, I hadn't seen people have sex before that close up. I mostly saw shadows and heard sounds behind walls in my house or at the nudist camp.

As an empath, I could feel the sexual attraction of my dad and uncle toward me and other women. My energy field was a sieve, worn down by constantly monitoring my environment. I had etheric cords connected to them and other adults around me. As an intuitive, I knew what types of thoughts they, as well as Gail, my aunt, and other adults around me, were thinking.

During this time of adolescence, my body was changing and the sexual tension and homelife stress caused me to have headaches every day. I hated that my body was becoming more womanly, knowing that I was becoming more and more sexually attractive.

The video confirmed and reinforced what I already knew about sex so far. It was only for self-gratification, not an act of love or caring. My uncle undressed me with his eyes and kissed me on the mouth inappropriately when he greeted me up to the point of this incident. He tried holding my hand whenever possible while walking in public, but at age 12 I finally had the guts to duck and weave and avoid those situations altogether. He got the memo.

My survival mechanisms kicked in when I asked my dad in desperation if I could move out that day. I knew not to ask for help from Stan since he behaved the same way that Glenn did. I did wonder if Stan would be upset or feel territorial about me, but I couldn't risk saying anything about the incident with Glenn. Stan had never intervened before with Gail's verbal abuse and her threats of hurting my dog.

Emboldened by my success in changing my situation, there was a small shift in my consciousness. While my foundational beliefs were still running the show, I began to advocate for myself a little more. Stan began to see that I saw right through his bullshit, much like Earl did back in Florida. Stan tried less often to pull one over on me or to get me to stroke his ego with tales of greatness from his real estate job. I was less enthusiastic about playing my old role in his world.

My arrested development pertaining to relationships and friendships prevented me from dating until after I got out of high school. I was pretty turned off by guys, which, in a way, protected me from further abuse and stress. I focused on just myself and on surviving my home life.

I found satisfaction in observing the teen world around me. I enjoyed throwing parties at my house when Stan and Gail were out of town and supporting my friends and their crush pursuits. I was thrilled to be a part of a group and to be included. I stayed closed off and intact, believing that I was not one of them and less than them. I felt happiest when things were under my control. I also never drank or smoked for the same reason. I was so turned off by those things because of my mother's smoking and drinking. Things could have gone way worse.

PTSD Is Real

The way I was able to heal was by treating the causes behind my anxiety, depression, and PTSD (post-traumatic stress disorder) from this event and others. The causes were my leaky and depleted energy fields, resulting in me not being grounded. Stress mode felt normal to me and was what I knew. These states depleted my body, mind, and energy resources, resulting in anxiety and nervousness all the time.

Learning to ground myself and to heal my energy field was my ticket to clearing my PTSD and chronic anxiety. I cleared decades-old residual resentment, bitterness, regret, self-hatred, and shame regarding my uncle and this traumatic event. I had to forgive myself for every bit it, as for a long time I had believed I was responsible for what happened.

I also had to clear beliefs about how to deal with this event before clearing the beliefs about the event itself:

◊ I have to stay angry, bitter, and resentful in order to be safe.

◊ Forgiveness means what they did was okay to do.

◊ Forgiveness is a sign of weakness.

◊ Showing anger shows strength.

These emotions were all rooted in fear. Love-based emotions, such as forgiveness, compassion, and gratitude, exist at higher frequencies (see Becoming Supernatural in the appendix). I fully healed by forgiving my uncle (and my dad and the others involved in this situation). I had to forgive through many layers of the onion over the years, as I evolved as a person, as I became a parent myself, and throughout my spiritual development.

High School

My first three years of high school were not great, but they weren't horrible either. I didn't walk out of there with a solid educational foundation. I got noticed by one of my teachers for performing well academically. This unknown teacher did not approach me, but they placed me in the gifted class for the following year. I was embarrassed and mortified by the attention I got from fellow students.

The California public school systems at that time (1979-1982) were among the worst in the nation. Teachers were on strike. Schools were stressed. Kids were disobedient and boisterous due to the conflict. Many teachers were disrespected by the students as lines were drawn. Teachers that chose to teach in spite of the strike (called scabs) were targeted.

I always loved school up to this point. My PTSD and anxiety were causing some chronic symptoms such as headaches, fatigue, and apathy. Energetically, school was now scary and stressful. I considered quitting but I listened to my intuition, which told me that I must finish high school. The idea of education as something sought-after and valuable was never discussed in my home. I didn't even know what college was until we had a speaker come talk to my school about majors. In spite of all of this, I knew that education was important, which was in alignment with how I felt about learning.

Our town—and the nation—was also distracted by Jimmy Carter and the Iran Hostage Crisis. Stan and Gail were riveted by the news and obsessively watched Walter Cronkite every night. I was triggered by the kidnapping from my personal experience and felt the harshness of the news flowing into the house. As an empath, I could feel what the hostages were feeling (scared, afraid for their lives, unsafe) simply by watching them on TV. Even though the situation was completely different, the association was never made by Stan or Gail that I might be upset by the news, especially seeing children crying for their parents. My friends at school talked about it nonstop too. We were all scared.

The core belief I reinforced in high school:

◊   The world is not safe.

New Freedoms

Even though those years lacked a foundation of family, nurturing, and safety, I experienced complete freedom. This freedom gave me a chance to experience some of aspects of normal adolescent growth and development. This freedom allowed me to develop without the filters of well-meaning parents and what they've taught me about the world I live in. Everything I knew came from what I experienced on my own, impartially and without the guidance and mentoring of my parents or other adults or teachers.

My mother, sister, and grandparents didn't visit, and neither did I. Florida was my past and my family there were also my past. I compartmentalized my emotions and thoughts about them and lost large blocks of memory.

School, going to friends' houses, and the horse barn were it for me. The horse barn probably saved my life. The time outside and with horses healed me. I could feel it but didn't know at the time why I felt the way I did. I just followed my desire to be with them. The sun, fresh air, exercise, horses, and safe friendships anchored me.

When I was home, I felt unsafe and out of place. I spent literally all of my time in my room listening to Judas Priest, Kansas, Van Halen, Journey, and Fleetwood Mac on my record player. I'd draw pictures of horses and copy album covers. I'd write letters to pass to my friends at school. I'd sometimes give my friend Lynn notes to read on our way to the horse barn. As time went on, I spent less time in the living room watching TV and more time alone. I surfaced to shower and eat, which went unnoticed by everyone.

Staying within the parameters of my beliefs about myself, I was satisfied with my social life. I felt grateful every day for being with the Parks and my other friends. But I also lived in fear, thinking that they could one day turn away from me, believing this could happen at any moment. Because of these beliefs, I was hyper-vigilant about being entertaining and helpful.

Lynn never spent time at my house, as she and my friends knew that I had a *weird dad*. It was common knowledge and I was okay with that, validating my own feelings. They'd laugh as they told me stories of seeing my dad in his robe, walking around on the front lawn doing chores or getting the newspaper. We lived on a main road that exited our neighborhood, so our house was driven by many, many times. I felt embarrassed, ashamed, and responsible for Stan's behavior, but found relief in their perspective and joined in making fun of him. I was mad at myself for not being able to find a clever way of getting him to stop.

I feared having anyone over because it was unpredictable, weird, and an unfriendly place to be. I was embarrassed by Stan and Gail and my home. All of my friends had bigger and nicer homes than me, reinforcing the belief that I was less than everyone else.

I didn't have a consistent, close group of school friends, as I seemed to wander in and out of various social groups. I was okay with that, as I had no expectations and didn't feel like I was entitled to those close friendships. Lynn was my security and foundation. I felt valued and that I served a purpose with Lynn and her family.

I was a floater at school. I was liked or at least tolerated by most of them, as I existed on the periphery and wasn't a threat in any way. I had no agenda and passed no unspoken judgement, so I was accepted. Even gang members felt comfortable with me, and I with them. Our school had a lot of gang activity, as well as regular fighting after school and in the halls. As a junior, I recall mainly having lunch with a couple of guy friends. I found it hard to find my footing and connect with the girls. I was shy, untrusting, and didn't offer much in my eyes. The guys were easier and more accepting.

One of the highlights was pool parties at Lynn's house. Lynn's family, especially her mom, was a bonus group for support and added to my feeling safe. She was always home and available in the background. Mrs. Park was a joy to be around, and Mr. and Mrs. Park became my role models as parents. Lynn had dogs, so we bonded over them too.

Here are my beliefs from this phase of my life:

- ◊ I have a weird dad which makes me weird.
- ◊ I am not good enough to have friends come over.
- ◊ My home and my life aren't good enough for others.
- ◊ Everyone knows my family is flawed and bad.
- ◊ I am not worthy of friendships because I am flawed and bad too.

Remembering Myself

In my 30s, I began the process of letting go of resentment, bitterness, and hatred toward my uncle (and my parents). I felt better and knew this was the way out. However, I didn't have the tools and knowledge then about replacing these thoughts and emotions with something better. As a result, I struggled with depression, which reinforced my beliefs:

- ◊ I am weak.
- ◊ I can't cope with life.

This paired "nicely" with postpartum depression and the lack of clarity I had about who I was.

I had my first year of spiritual awakening in my 40s. It was all about tackling self-love. The core belief *there's something wrong with me* was a tough one to crack. It was like a large boulder blocking my stream of self-love. How could I love myself when I'm such a freak? I am the daughter of two people with major problems who did terrible things to me. I couldn't even look in the mirror because I was constantly reminded of Stan. I looked so much like him. Every day I stoked the fires of my hatred toward myself because of my physical appearance. I kept the vibration active and my neural circuits firing away. I could not love what I hated.

So, my healing really began as baby steps in entertaining the idea of liking physical aspects of myself. My large chin from Stan's side of the family was a huge preoccupation in high school. I spent hours daydreaming of plastic surgery to fix my chin and my face so I would lose all resemblance of my father.

Self-love seemed like a silly concept. I thought it was ridiculous to love things that I wanted to change about myself. As I learned more about energy and how unprocessed thoughts, memories, and emotions get stored in the body and cause blocks, it all became clear. These blocks caused unwanted chronic conditions like my PTSD and anxiety. I had to full-on figure out this self-love stuff.

Months of working on myself every day helped me identify and clear these beliefs I had about myself. It took me a long time to establish a foothold in thinking new thoughts about myself. It was awkward and uncomfortable the entire time, until about nine months had passed—the same amount of time as human gestation. This synchronicity is noted. Reiki self-treatments, Accunect balancing, one-hour walking meditations four days a week, and applying the concepts of spiritual and energy healing books were also part of my day.

By the end of those nine months, my spiritual practice was part of my morning routine as much as brushing my teeth. My energy and thoughts about myself were finally part of the solution, not part of the problem. I became—and still am today—my own best friend.

Living with the Parks (Junior Year)

Stan got a new engineering job down in Los Angeles during the last few months of my junior year in high school. He became disenchanted with real estate and the ever-fluctuating market. I am stressed about moving in general, but also feel a little relief and excitement about Los Angeles. Intuitively, it feels like my life will greatly improve even though I have never been there. I am hopeful that I will belong there.

Stressed about school, I propose that I live with the Parks (if they will take me in) to finish out my junior year. They have a guest bedroom and I know they like me a lot. I am nervous about ruining the friendship by asking, but if they say no, I will be moving anyway. Stan doesn't seem to care whether I stay with them or move with him, so I ask the Parks and they say yes. Stan talks to them and gives them a small amount of money for food and gas. I am horrified by his cheap offer, but I have no power to change it and the Parks agree to it.

Stan drops me off with my things and my dog Shawna. He turns off the engine when we pull up to their house and turns to me. *He changed his mind, I knew it!* He is shifting awkwardly in his seat, about to say something. My heart starts racing. Thoughts about how to beef up my case for staying with the Parks floods my mind. My stomach is clenched and filled with butterflies.

"You know, I'm actually SAD to leave you here," Stan says, surprised himself by what he has just said. He excitedly points to one small tear forming in the corner of his right eye.

I say nothing, scared of what he's going to say next.

"Look! I'm even crying over leaving you here," he says, frustrated now that I'm not jumping up and down impressed. I watch his tear, anticipating it to fall onto his cheek but it stays.

I look down at my dog and pat her on the head.

"Give me a hug," he says, leaning halfway toward me. I quickly do what he says, leaning over and bracing for his arm to circle around me.

"See you later," I say as I slam the heavy Cadillac door. I climb the steps to the very top quickly so I can turn around and make sure he drives away. I am breathing so hard and sweating. He slowly drives off, leaning forward to fiddle with the radio. *Oh my god, I actually pulled this off! I am free of him!* I have never seen him cry before, even though it was about his loss, not about mine or my welfare. I am leaving Stan behind, but now I'm nervous approaching the Parks' front door with my purse and my suitcase. I am never nervous at their house. This is a new situation. I'm living here as a guest. I can't believe they are actually letting me stay!

I loved staying there. I found ways to be helpful and to complete my self-prescribed duties of being a jokester and being agreeable to Lynn's every preference. I followed her around like a puppy. She once got annoyed by me and told me to stop following her around the house. She had become my new barometer of normality, replacing Stan and Gail. I quickly realized it was wrong and had encroached on Lynn's healthy boundaries. I began to calm myself down, trying not to be so fearful. I was on alert about acting a certain way or missing social cues.

I never told Lynn, the Parks, or anyone from that time about my abuse or neglect. The kidnapping story was something I shared with a lot of people though! I got a lot of attention from telling it. It was a way for me to connect to people. I didn't have very good social skills, obviously.

Here are the beliefs I created during this time:

- ◊ My childhood was not normal at all.
- ◊ The Parks are a normal family who I get to observe and learn from.

Realizing I Have Major Issues

Not being present in my body or grounded in general was the main cause behind my anxiety and social stress. I acted like my father when I felt uncomfortable in social situations. I loved to tell big stories and be entertaining. I savored every moment of positive feedback from people. This was the way I knew how to connect to other people. Looking back, this awareness sickened me. I betrayed myself by emulating what I hated. As I became grounded and spent more time living in my body and having positive social experiences, I lost my habit of showing off and being entertaining to feel safe. I felt like I could be myself and not have to be responsible for being "on," helpful, or responsible for others. I practiced learning healthy behaviors from new people around me.

Trying Something New

Bonding with friends in college who had experienced similar trauma empowered me to turn the blame away from me and onto my parents and other abusers. Sending judgement and rage toward the responsible people gave me a lot of relief. I became confrontational and judgmental of every abuser. Once I did this, I felt like I was more equal to people. I felt like I deserved more from friends and people around me. I wouldn't feel *equal* and *worthy* until my 40s, when I began my spiritual development, but it was a healthy start.

~ Four ~

Belief Theme:
Regiment of Responsibility

4: Regiment of Responsibility

It was up to me and only me to not mess up. My family's safety was solely in my hands. I could not trust anyone else, even my husband, to make things better. Anything bad that happens is a result of me not anticipating or preventing it. My childhood conditioning resulted in me coming up with this subconscious belief that I was responsible for literally everything:

I am responsible for:

- ◊ The safety of others around me.
- ◊ All of the bad things that happened to me and my sister.
- ◊ The moods and stress levels of my mother.
- ◊ The moods and preferences of my father.
- ◊ My children.
- ◊ The well-being of other people's children.
- ◊ Convincing parents to adopt the new health paradigm.
- ◊ Being on alert at all times.
- ◊ Uplifting my parents and others to feel better.

- ◊ Being here to serve and entertain.
- ◊ Proving my value over and over.

My Young Adult Years (1990 – 1997)

After I graduated from college, I met my soulmate and future husband Burt and my soulmate BFF Teri through my job in advertising. Work culture matched my lack of self-esteem and feelings of unworthiness, but also included people who were extroverts and fun and curious about the broad view of the world. I loved the fast-paced cutting-edge environment and being on the pulse of the economy.

While the media business was such a great fit for my interests, it wasn't a good fit for my sensitivities and unprocessed baggage. Since I was subconsciously working from my beliefs that I was just a weak person lacking coping skills, my work stress broke me down physically. Unbeknownst to me at the time, I was absorbing the stress and all the low-vibration thoughts and feelings around me. I couldn't tell what was generated by me and what was coming from my coworkers and the toxicity of the building.

Harsh modern living conditions were at an all-time high as I was exposed to computers generating very strong and noticeable heat, beaming straight at me from about a foot away. Harsh bright lights and offices located on a high floor left me in a perpetual state of ungroundedness. The workplace conditions of the late '80s and early '90s were often like this.

Chainsmokers, including my boss who smoked all day just a few feet from me, were the norm. The smoke reminded me of my mother's cigarette habit, triggering learned helplessness, basic apathy, and disconnection from myself. I willingly viewed my job as a sentence, not questioning how to get out of these bad conditions. My peers also had these beliefs and we reinforced each other.

My nervous system was always on alert, further conditioned by the intense advertising environment. My ungroundedness led to panicky thoughts and episodes on a weekly basis while working under hard deadlines and long hours. I began to lose my hair. My periods were horrible and erratic.

Chronic fatigue, chronic anxiety, and feeling warm and clammy became my norm. My food intake became erratic. I reverted back to my childhood survival mode, ignoring my own needs and desires, and instead giving up my power to my work environment and the desires of coworkers and authority figures.

These were all subconscious decisions and choices that I made based on my core beliefs. I even took a job that was perfect on paper, ignoring the glaring red flags about the volatile and emotionally abusive new boss. Subconsciously, his energy resonated with my programming.

After all, my beliefs were:

◊ I am not worthy.

◊ I am responsible for the well-being of everyone around me.

◊ I have to suffer to succeed.

When I could, I took dance classes in the evenings to alleviate stress and do something I enjoyed. I returned to taking long walks in the Santa Monica Canyon.

I began to desire more things in life. I wanted more family and sought out people to build community and connection. I began to see what I didn't have and wanted it too. I felt wronged by life and betrayed by my parents for not providing these things. I felt entitled to friends and love and went after it like a bull in a china shop, often looking in the wrong places or having unrealistic expectations. These desires clashed with my programming, which said:

◊ I am here to serve others.

◊ Other people know more than me.

◊ Other people are better than me; I am damaged goods.

Anger was my healing fuel for the next couple of decades. I acted out by standing up to guys at bars and in social situations.

I was empowered by the support of my friends, my belief of feeling responsible for them, and I raised awareness about how messed up my childhood was and how badly women are treated.

I sought out platonic friendships with men, finding them safer and easier to handle than friendships with women. I was interested in dating, but I wasn't obsessed like a typical young person might be at this phase of life.

Confrontation became a "thing" for me. I enjoyed the adrenaline rush of yelling at guys who stared openly at me or my friends. I'd be close to physically attacking them. All of the suppressed anger I had inside me from Stan and Glenn had an outlet. Even though this wasn't an ideal way to deal with my emotions, it helped. I still used my skills cultivated by the culture at the time too. I knew how to behave and to execute my role of diffusing and redirecting come-ons or inappropriate behavior and how to get out of dangerous situations (more on this in Part 5).

As I experimented outside of living in fear, I was able to access love-based emotions and learn to trust a few friends who were male and also to successfully cultivate dating relationships. I was always mindful of my twisted thinking about sex in our culture and in my relationships. I was able to fully embrace intimacy in a healthy way by compartmentalizing my childhood traumas. Amazingly, I had several successful relationships and eventually married. I was able to maintain long-term friendships.

Breaking Down

Things had to get really bad in order for me to face these beliefs about being responsible for everyone's well-being at work, including being responsible for the verbal abuse, bad behavior, and terrible working conditions. My PTSD had gotten so bad at my last advertising job that I finally quit. I felt like a failure and incompetent for not being able to control and improve my situation, or that of the others around me. I was at a new low.

Facing My Fears

My healing began by hitting rock bottom. I finally listened to the feedback about my bad work situation from my friends and fiancé. I deserved respect and a positive work environment. I finally believed it and quit my job. It was scary not to have a plan or know what I'd be doing next, but I was miserable enough to try something different. The belief that I needed to have a clear and predictable career path was out of my control, making me miserable.

Here are the beliefs that were running the show:

- ◊ I have to be in control.
- ◊ My life is chaotic.
- ◊ I am inadequate.
- ◊ I am not worthy.

I created new beliefs in my 40s. Here are some of the first new beliefs I adopted so I could be more receptive to intuitive guidance:

- ◊ It is safe to let go.
- ◊ Life loves me.
- ◊ All is well.
- ◊ I am a divine child of Source energy.

Marriage and Family (1997 – 2011)

As my relationship with my fiancé began to grow, I realized for the first time that I wanted to have children. Because of my worthiness issues (among others), I couldn't believe that he loved me. We got married after four years of dating. I was so grateful and amazed. Up to this point in my life, I couldn't imagine myself as a mother. I also didn't want to pass down damaged genes.

As I reflect back, I had so many unprocessed emotions toward my parents and myself. Hatred, anger, grief, sadness, despair, hopelessness, and so on. These unprocessed emotions, along with the beliefs I created, had limited my desires for my future up to this point.

In spite of my conditioning, something inside me turned on (perhaps my DNA telling me it's time) and my intuition began to entertain the idea of children. I felt a tiny bit of hope inside that maybe I would turn out okay, like maybe I could be a normal person. After all, this wonderful ("normal") man loved me and wanted to have children with me. I was hoping his DNA would be stronger than mine so our children would be healthy and happy.

I decided that I needed to consider other careers that would work better for me as a parent. I decided to go back to school to become a physical therapist. I had always been interested in the medical field and working in PT could offer flexibility in setting my own hours around my parental needs.

All my desires began to come to the surface. I wanted my children to be surrounded by nature and have access to horses and pets. I wanted it for me too. I wanted a safe partner who was solid and who I could rely on. Like with many people, I wanted the opposite experience from what I'd had for my children. I modeled myself after the Moores and the Parks and others who had made an impression.

We settled into our family life and had two kids. I couldn't look back on my relationship with my mom or my own experiences growing up. Since I was never close to my mother, I didn't really know what I was supposed to do. My mother kept to herself and didn't talk much about her own childhood. Her disabilities were likely a huge obstacle to having a normal childhood. I can now see she must be a resilient and smart person to live in the typical world, graduating college, marrying, and even teaching piano when she had a hearing impairment. I know that her lineage gave me some of my hardiness and strength. I will never know what she went through, but I respect and appreciate the positive qualities that I inherited from her.

I learned on my own how to cook and raise a baby by reading books and talking to other moms. It was a very lonely, dark time for me. My anxiety and depression were at an all-time high. I struggled with fitting in and finding close friends because of my beliefs and because New England was so different culturally.

Even though feeling isolated and different was normal for me, I had a new, stronger motivation to find community and normalcy. This happened organically through my crazy drive to be the perfect mother. Like many mothers, I wanted to give my children the perfect life.

When my first child was diagnosed with numerous health problems, I didn't experience disbelief or spend time thinking "why me?" like many parents do. I responded the way I normally did, with PTSD symptoms of anxiety and fatigue.

I became hyper-vigilant about the kids, often sleeping on the floor of my children's bedroom out of fear for their safety. I also fit the stereotype of the helicopter parent of the 2000s. This was all part of a culture that I believe happened because of our harsh modern living conditions. More than ever before, families were being raised in isolation. The cumulative toxic burden from the environment and our food supply triggered many parents to feel the same way I did: unsafe. Things were not right. *Our DNA knew that our living conditions were not good.*

I had paranoid thoughts about Stan spontaneously showing up at my house or school so that "Grandpa could take the kids out to lunch." I worried about my kids getting hurt by child predators. I was obsessed with the sex offender registry and monitoring the behavior of adults in the park. I was hyper-vigilant about my children leaving my sight anywhere ever. I was super focused and militant in every way, including providing the very best food, experiences, and overall care for them. I was able to recreate a better outcome than I was able to do for my sister.

My beliefs set me up to anticipate problems:

- ◊ Life is dangerous.
- ◊ Someone kidnapping my children is a reality.
- ◊ I am damaged goods, so I expect health problems.
- ◊ Life is hard.
- ◊ Nothing comes easy.
- ◊ I am responsible for my children's health problems.
- ◊ It is my responsibility to fix other people's problems.
- ◊ I am weak and unable to cope with regular life.

Healing My Children

My crazy childhood conditioned me to question the status quo, authority, and the beliefs I saw around me. My experiences taught me that *authority can't be trusted*. I didn't believe people ever had my best interest or my child's best interest in mind. I intrinsically knew there had to be answers for my children's chronic health conditions. I didn't see anyone getting better around me and felt like I was living a scene from the story "The Emperor's New Clothes." My "I don't belong" belief made it okay to break away from what my mommy friends were doing and to search for answers.

Through my searches, I connected with parents and practitioners who found success in treating the causes behind the numerous symptoms our children had. A comprehensive, individualized, and multidisciplinary program of nutrient-dense food, green living, detoxification, and therapy helped my children get back into balance.

I dedicated all of my time, thoughts, and effort toward finding solutions and supporting their healing. All of that unprocessed Anger was my fuel and it came pouring out. I was pissed and it felt good! I lived off the adrenaline high. I was out of control and a bit unstable as I was living in a depleted, toxic body I was ignoring.

As unhealthy as it was to use anger and pure rage at the situation and the betrayal of our medical system, it did help me heal. I found courage, my voice, and new ways to use my business knowledge, experience, and sensitivities to my advantage. I could read teachers, attorneys, doctors, and scientists easily. My B.S. meter was incredible.

Even though I was successfully navigating the scaffolding we have today for a healthcare system, I gave away all of my power to my children. They were my new barometer for health and normalcy, just like my parents had been for me when I was a child. I familiarly slipped into this role as I could empathically feel and know how to help my children. I could anticipate their needs and wants like mothers do, but also in an intense and unhealthy helicopter-ish way.

As an empath, I just knew instantly what was working and what wasn't. I knew who to call and what to try. My belief that *I am responsible* for the wellness of my children was my guide. I was also driven by my belief that *the world is not safe.*

My children were born at the beginning of the big wave of the epidemic of childhood chronic conditions that we see today. The "new normal" of asthma, allergies, autism, ADHD, learning delays and disorders, autoimmune conditions, etc. I was capable of embracing the unknown because I knew the known was bad news! My husband always referred to me as the biggest skeptic he'd ever met.

Here are the beliefs I created:

◊ Pediatricians and neurologists know nothing.

◊ Medical people and their militant, antiquated complacent stance is responsible for this epidemic.

◊ There are answers out there in the unknown.

◊ I am responsible for finding those answers.

◊ I am capable of researching, vetting, and implementing integrative protocols focused on causes.

◊ I am responsible for educating and persuading medical professionals to change.

◊ I am responsible for educating and persuading other parents to live holistically by eating clean and living green.

◊ It is not safe to ask for help.

I have no words to describe my gratitude for my warrior mom tribe and the healthcare practitioners who brought healing and a reversal of chronic conditions so that my children could live happy, healthy lives. I am also thankful to my wonderful husband, who believed in me and brought us the funds day after day so I could be pissed off searching, buying books, and flying to classes to learn.

The gift of No Guidance

As the years went by, my beliefs were still intact but the trauma of healing my children was less raw. I became more relaxed when I talked to other parents. I didn't worry about other people's children as much as I used to. I learned that people have their own path and that they may or may not get to the same place we were in overcoming blocks to healing. I realized how limited many parents were due to influences and beliefs they acquired from their own parents and childhoods. Many parents with medical people in the family had a tough time overcoming the conventional health paradigm so that they could find their unique path to healing.

I learned that parents don't always put their children first or do what they know is right to do. This happens when their own personal beliefs get in the way. I learned that I could absorb and apply new knowledge and tools more easily than many parents could. This was a gift. I remembered feeling smart when I was a kid and teachers placed me in gifted classes and asked to get my I.Q. tested. My parents were disinterested, so these accolades didn't take hold in my identity or raise my self-esteem. But then I was ready to consider that I was smart and capable! I realized not everyone has the ability to see how their own stuff can block healing for their children. I realized it was unhealthy to make my children my barometer, even though it felt right to me to always put them first.

Here are the beliefs I created:

- ◊ I allow other parents to follow their own path toward healing.

- ◊ I practice detached compassion toward parents struggling with limiting conditions toward healing.

- ◊ I trust that the Universe will provide the right healing at the right time for each child.
- ◊ I am smart and capable.

~ Five ~

Belief Theme:
The Patriarchy

5: The Patriarchy

I want to say upfront that I have forgiven my dad, my mother, my aunt and uncle, my grandparents, the men who molested me, the men who disrespected me, the men who abused me, and those who have made me feel unsafe over the course of my life. I forgave all of the boys who came up to me from behind in a crowd during rock concerts and felt me up, their hands wildly groping my crotch and my breasts, surprising me and tipping me off balance before disappearing back into the crowd.

Most importantly, I've forgiven myself for feeling responsible for this ungodly behavior and for playing the role of the oppressed female.

I'm no saint. It's taken a lot of elbow grease, crying, and investment emotionally, physically, and financially. It's taken action steps and daily work to figure this stuff out, piece by piece. Forgiving these people is just that: forgiveness. I did much of this forgiveness in my own mind, not in person. I didn't need to be in front of them physically to heal. In many cases, it was not safe or appropriate to do this in person. I have also forgiven people that have passed away. Their soul connection to me has received this healing.

I know that these people weren't born with an agenda to hurt me. They all have their own karma and beliefs, their own paths that they have chosen to follow. I have learned to practice detached compassion toward them. Some days, it's not so easy.

The all-powerful institution of patriarchy taught my parents and all the women I've come across that women are second class citizens.

That we are not as smart. A 2017 study* demonstrated that by age six, girls believe that boys are smarter, and that they change their behavior to accommodate this knowledge about their world.

My own family taught me all about what it meant to be female, starting with those photoshoots as a preschooler. My environment and family taught me these beliefs about women and men:

- ◊ Women are not safe.
- ◊ Women compete with me.
- ◊ Women serve others.
- ◊ Women serve men as objects of pleasure.
- ◊ Women don't feel good about themselves.
- ◊ There is no comradery with other women.
- ◊ Being threatened, molested, or assaulted is par for the course.

---

* "Gender stereotypes about intellectual ability emerge early and influence children's interests," *Science,* Jan 2017, Vol. 355, Issue 6323, pp. 389-391

Trump Is My Dad

Okay, *technically* he's not, but his personality and mental disabilities are cut from the same cloth. As we all know, the world changed when he took office. In addition to the usual complaints, worries, and fears, Trump changed me on a deep, emotional level for the better. He turned out to be the symbol that triggered many core beliefs that I didn't even know I had (or thought I had healed). He represented Stan in all of his glory and he was everywhere I looked and heard. I could not escape "my dad" even if I tried!

I knew that I had to get busy applying BeliefWork and energy healing tools stat... or else. Not only for me, but for my children. I had to be their rock and guide through this mess.

During his first speech as president-elect, decades-old feelings of unworthiness, self-hatred, rejection of myself and my feminine side, and sexual trauma all came tumbling out of their hiding places from deep inside me. I was surprised and horrified by these feelings. I had gotten used to feeling pretty good, as I had done so much work on myself and felt like I had a handle on where I was and what I wanted. All of that went out the window.

Intuitively, I knew that Obama was going to be our last "normal" president, and I sensed a big catalyst for change was coming. I remember telling my husband, "this is it," after he was elected the second time. I would have preferred a gentler wake-up call, but I know that the Universe is giving us what we've asked for in order for us to evolve and move forward. Trump gives us what we need to expose and dissolve these antiquated paradigms (not just politics, but religion, education, nationalism, and our medical system, to name a few that just don't fit the bill anymore). I mean, is there anyone today who believes that these systems are working well?

Trump has symbolically forced our hand. We are forced to talk about the taboo subjects of politics and religion. We are forced to communicate rather than to live in fear in our own bubbles and to abide by old ways that once helped humans survive and procreate. I feel like we are in the middle of a 1.0, working toward a 2.0 upgrade. The Age of Aquarius as they say, as it's not a new concept. I can feel, see, and know this to be true. Our deepest and darkest subconscious beliefs as a collective conscious have been in the spotlight ever since he was elected. So much has been written about this so I leave the analysis to the experts, but I wanted to set the framework for my personal impact into context.

The pussy tape exposé was the epiphany where I realized that, wow, he is really going to win. I saw fellow females on TV enamored with Trump and loving everything he said and did. I saw them butter him up, play to his ego, and find him charismatic. I saw them relate to him as something familiar in their lives. It's what they know.

I saw myself in those followers, remembering that I was once one of them. My beliefs caused me to act the way they did as a child and young adult. I abided by the ebb and flow and every whim of Stan, of male authority figures, and of men (and boys) in general. I knew how to feed an ego regularly and to be provocative when I was subconsciously prompted to. I knew how to placate men.

I wasn't *great* at it, as my disdain would become apparent. I'd sit stoically as demeaning jokes and manhandling took place. I did the bare minimum, as anger would often rise inside me, causing me to crack just a little. I did manage to be mostly "good" and knew how to not make waves. Ulcers, headaches, anxiety, and general stress were my normal and they were the symptoms of my misalignment with who I really was inside.

I left my higher self alone and shut off from the physical world because that was how I chose to survive in order to have peace and safety. It wasn't a conscious decision that I made to behave in this manner. It was how I learned to behave that worked. Every day of my childhood I witnessed this paradigm work for Stan and the majority of men during that era. I saw my mother, aunt, and other women in our family (including me) tolerate Stan's "huckster" and "chauvinist" ways. Both of these terms were self-proclaimed and viewed as positive attributes.

The '60s and '70s patriarchal belief system was hardwired. I totally believed it to the core for a long time, until I became a young adult and learned new ways to live, communicate, and allow my true self to shine. I have witnessed other women my age do the same, while others chose to be loyal to their men, affirming their choices and those beliefs. Some chose the status quo out of fear of the unknown or a lack of feminine kinship.

Like many people, I found my way through the horror of the news each day. Trump as a symbol of my dad (and childhood and core beliefs) was there taking center stage. Each day, I examined my feelings. I had to because I knew from experience that facing my fears and clearing them gave me more peace and joy. I wasn't ever going to go back to a limited life ruled by my past. Like going to the gym, I knew the payoff.

I exercised my right to my feelings and let them be heard, but I also remembered that these emotions were a barometer of my own normalcy. I took back the power I gave to the news outlets. I had wanted them to be my authority, believing they knew more than my own inner being. But I remembered that only I can contribute to the outcome of how my life plays out.

Today, I can glance at a photo in my social media feed or see Trump on TV without being triggered by addressing the core beliefs he activated. Because of Trump, I was able to forgive Stan and my mother for who they were and for the pain and suffering they caused. I *thought* I had forgiven them completely and wholeheartedly and had cleared the beliefs associated with them, but a core layer resonated and had an opportunity to be heard.

Because of this deep BeliefWork, Trump no longer triggers fear, hate, or anger like he once did. Neither do his followers or their beliefs. I recognize and accept their path and see the beliefs that run their lives. Because I see them, it is easier for me to find acceptance and to feel detached compassion for them. They are my greatest teachers as I move toward more awakening. Don't get the wrong idea though: I sometimes get derailed by yet another low in the news cycle, but I find it easier and easier to get myself back into balance. I have a right to these emotions, as they are the truth about what I see going on in the world. When I feel unwanted emotions that are pretty strong, I ask questions such as these:

- ◊ What emotions am I feeling?
- ◊ Why am I feeling this way?
- ◊ What belief do I have that's causing me to feel this emotion?
- ◊ What conditions do I need to let go of in order to feel safe?
- ◊ What beliefs do I need to let go of in order to feel safe?
- ◊ What beliefs do I need to let go of in order to love and accept myself?
- ◊ Who do I need to feel compassion for?

Slowly but surely, my dedicated spiritual practice uncovered beliefs that were causing my newfound feelings triggered by seeing "my dad" on TV. I followed Louise Hay's advice and began forgiving others for not being the way I wanted them to be. I uncovered conditions I'd placed on life in order to be happy.

I recognize that we all want the same things in life and that they are me and I am them. We are a mirror of each other. We are one, an unbreakable connection as lifeforms on this planet.

Self-care, facing my fears, and remembering that fear is just an emotion have been my daily practice. Tapping out memories and emotions and using other energy medicine tools has been key in healing. I created new beliefs based on how I wanted to feel and what I wanted in life:

Old Beliefs

- ◊ I am not worthy.
- ◊ I am flawed.
- ◊ There is something wrong with me.
- ◊ I am less than.
- ◊ My life is chaos.
- ◊ I have no control over my life.
- ◊ Women have no power.
- ◊ I am powerless.
- ◊ Sex is a perversion.
- ◊ Women are here to serve men.
- ◊ I can't express myself.
- ◊ The world is not safe.
- ◊ There is no meaning to life.

New Beliefs

- ◊ I am safe.
- ◊ It is safe to feel these fears.
- ◊ I don't need these fears to be safe.
- ◊ I can let go of this pattern.
- ◊ I am worthy.
- ◊ I am a divine child of God.

- I am powerful.
- I am confident and capable.
- I am perfect just as I am.
- I create my own reality.
- Life loves me.
- The Universe has my back.
- Being feminine is fun.
- Expressing my sexuality is safe.
- Expressing my femininity is safe.
- I speak clearly and easily with my authentic voice.
- I know what it feels like to be heard.
- People like me.
- I know what it feels like to be me.

Old Beliefs

- ◊ I am not worthy.
- ◊ I am flawed.
- ◊ There is something wrong with me.
- ◊ I am less than.
- ◊ My life is chaos.
- ◊ I have no control over my life.
- ◊ Women have no power.
- ◊ I am powerless.
- ◊ Sex is a perversion.
- ◊ Women are here to serve men.
- ◊ I can't express myself.
- ◊ The world is not safe.
- ◊ There is no meaning to life.

New Beliefs

- ◊ I am safe.
- ◊ It is safe to feel these fears.
- ◊ I don't need these fears to be safe.
- ◊ I can let go of this pattern.
- ◊ I am worthy.
- ◊ I am a divine child of God.

- ◊ I am powerful.
- ◊ I am confident and capable.
- ◊ I am perfect just as I am.
- ◊ I create my own reality.
- ◊ Life loves me.
- ◊ The Universe has my back.
- ◊ Being feminine is fun.
- ◊ Expressing my sexuality is safe.
- ◊ Expressing my femininity is safe.
- ◊ I speak clearly and easily with my authentic voice.
- ◊ I know what it feels like to be heard.
- ◊ People like me.
- ◊ I know what it feels like to be me.

The Ford/Kavanaugh chaos

I am one of the many women and men that has experienced sexual abuse and objectification. Like many women growing up in the patriarchal system of the '60s and '70s, I accepted the subconscious programming of how to behave and what to accept as normal in order to survive. Taking cues modeled by my family and community, I learned how to diffuse and fake laughter at inappropriate behavior. I became savvy at foreseeing, avoiding, and getting out of risky situations. There were no adult females around to help me or resources to talk to, as things were happening inside the house right in front of them. They were doing the same thing I was, navigating around as best they could. Even today, these topics are taboo.

People say, "It is what it is."

But is it?

With all of the tools and knowledge we have today, I believe that the Ford/Kavanaugh chaos is forcing our hand to make a choice: Hang on to the patriarchal, sexist paradigm that clearly doesn't fit with today's world or take this opportunity to heal.

Why is it hard for people to change in general, let alone to change a belief system and the only way of living they've ever known? We humans are designed to reject anything that defies core beliefs and values, both good and not so good. It's a survival mechanism. How many times have you heard a person from an older generation say, "It's just what we did back then."

Thinking differently about tolerated sexual abuse from long ago challenges the validity of our way of living. People don't like making mistakes or thinking they made them in the past, even with new information. People think that deep reflection and unwanted emotions are better to be avoided: phew! Emotions such as shame, blame, guilt, and resentment, or mixed emotions about our loved ones, are no fun. We don't want to threaten our core programming, and life goes on without expansion or progress toward evolving.

Fundamental beliefs and ideas—both the good stuff and the not so good stuff—are programmed by age 11. Good values are virtues we learned from our family, religion, and community, such as compassion, generosity, honesty, tolerance, and patience. Unwanted values such as discrimination, sexism, expectations of others, fears about the world, and beliefs that limit us from our potential are also incorporated into who we become at a young age.

Anger about questioning the status quo is normal and a good sign. It means your gut instinct, your higher self, isn't in alignment with what you believe. Accepting a new way of thinking in order to expand and evolve doesn't come easy. We have to coax our original programming into accepting the new software. It is similar to the error message we get on our computers: "You are about to download something from the Internet. It may be malware".

Programming that has been triggered by the Kavanaugh proceedings sheds light on all of that stuff we subconsciously dealt with and tucked away as, "It is what it is." Many people are realizing they've been treated like an object and have put up with dangerous and inappropriate sexual behavior their entire life, that they've given away their power. It's especially hard when these men or women are loved ones.

"You've been living in a dream world, Neo." It's scary and as time goes by, it's not as malleable for change.

What I am here to tell you is that you can heal yourself and future generations by changing your programming. Maya Angelou says it best: "Do the best you can until you know better. Then when you know better, do better."

You are smart and capable. Take some time to sit with yourself in a neutral, nonjudgmental way. Really listen to your heart and what you know is true for you.

Here are some questions to ask yourself:

- ◊ What emotions am I feeling?
- ◊ Why am I feeling this way?
- ◊ What belief do I have that's causing me to feel this emotion?
- ◊ Who do I need to forgive?
- ◊ What do I need to let go of?
- ◊ What conditions do I need to let go of in order to feel safe?
- ◊ What beliefs do I need to let go of in order to feel safe?
- ◊ What beliefs do I need to let go of in order to love and accept myself?
- ◊ Who do I need to feel compassion for?

Here are some common beliefs to reconsider:

- ◊ I am not worthy.
- ◊ I have no control over my life.
- ◊ Women have no power.
- ◊ I am powerless.
- ◊ Women are here to serve men.
- ◊ I can't express myself.
- ◊ It is not safe to be angry.

- ◊ The world is not safe.
- ◊ There is no meaning to life.
- ◊ No one will help me.
- ◊ I am not able to receive.

Here are some new beliefs to replace the old paradigms:

- ◊ I am safe.
- ◊ It is safe to feel these fears.
- ◊ I do not need these fears to be safe.
- ◊ I can let go of this pattern.
- ◊ I am worthy.
- ◊ I am powerful.
- ◊ I am confident and capable.
- ◊ I speak clearly and easily with my authentic voice.
- ◊ I know what it feels like to be heard.
- ◊ I know what it feels like to be me.

You deserve the utmost peace and happiness this world experience has to offer. Freedom is waiting for you.

Epilogue

As I write this epilogue, it's early fall in 2020. The new normal is here to stay—we're adapting to the impact of the coronavirus pandemic and buckling up for the presidential election. I'm sure you can guess who I am voting for, but our antiquated systems of society still require the same repair work no matter what administration is in office. I'm sitting here at home feeling extremely fortunate, with a roof over my head and jobs that support our family.

At the beginning of this traumatic year, I recognized myself in the shell-shocked faces around me and in the media. I saw myself in friends, acquaintances, strangers—as their anger and frustration grew along with their awareness. The knowledge that our authority figures don't have solid answers, that they can't ensure our safety, was growing.

To my relief, the truth about the medical paradigm is finally being seen by those who have been jolted awake by the pandemic. I feel hope as I witness the general public question a possible vaccine and the medical authorities' message. People are thinking twice about our manufacturers' default response: "Pay no attention to the man behind the curtain." For the first time, many are doing their homework and not taking things at face value.

It's thrilling to see people take stock of what they are eating and their lifestyle habits. People are finally learning about their own immune system. I'm inspired by the conversations I never thought in a million years I'd be having with people about food quality, supplements, and toxins. These conversations had only ever happened among those in the chronic illness world, those who had already left mainstream medicine. Never before had I imagined that people were going to make connections between chronic conditions or symptoms and their vulnerability to this virus. It's not just me; I now have company!

COVID-19 is forcing everyone to realize that every person on this planet is connected and impacted by what others do and the choices they make. The perception of separateness is dissolving. The health and well-being of someone living across the globe matters to everyone! The choices they make matter even more.

COVID-19 has also exposed how sick we truly are as a society. The one-size-fits-all, pharmaceutical-controlled medical system sucks. We have an opportunity to become vibrant, resilient, and healthy—with new paradigms to replace the old ones, the ones that applied to a world that existed long ago.

As I illustrated in my chapter about marriage and family, I went through this transition to awareness when I was fueled by the desire to help my children. I feel ahead of the game because of it, as now I can share my world with everyone. I feel more a part of the world than I ever have.

The pandemic's reboot has offered me relief. Now, every day I wake up feeling hopeful. I no longer go about my day responding to my environment thinking thoughts like "This is not sustainable" or "When will this momentum stop?" My kids' generation is more entitled and empowered than ever to question authority, to stand up for Mother Earth, and to stand up for themselves.

I am humbled by and grateful for the sacrifices people have made in some way as a result of COVID-19, especially in the most vulnerable and resource-poor communities and by those who have been kept apart from loved ones. The limitations and insidious nature of mainstream medicine is heartbreaking. The inequities highlight even more suffering in the most vulnerable populations as the economy falls apart.

There's too much to comment on as we discover the unraveling and exposure of our many antiquated, debilitating systems. However, I do want to acknowledge my perspective as a white woman of privilege. It is up to me to educate myself and to make changes in order for our world to grow and heal. It's up to me to hold space for my clients. It's up to me to educate, support, and model behavior for my children. It's up to me to understand how we got here, why racism continues to flourish, and how to connect with my own personal racism and clear it (BeliefWork comes in handy here).

Robin DiAngelo's book White Fragility: Why It's So Hard for White People to Talk About Racism gave me the knowledge and tools to talk about white fragility with my family, friends, and others around me as I navigate this new normal. These are intense conversations and each one of us holds a different perspective. I have so much more to learn and am learning more each day. My bookshelf is yet again growing on a new topic for me, but one that has been a harsh everyday reality that people of color have lived with their entire lives.

As always, there's work to do on myself to address these emotions and face my beliefs. I could write another book just on how much I've taken for granted, how much opportunity and free passes I've been granted because of how I look. I have felt so motivated and emboldened to find a way to be of service as a white person and to do better learning about microaggressions and other habits I was unaware of.

My hope is that a new paradigm is being built around these glaring ongoing systemic problems. Just like with COVID-19, I am grateful to those who have sacrificed so much for this movement. I am grateful for the shifts that have taken place, especially in seeing white people take greater responsibility for this work.

My Vision of the Future

I envision governments spending billions of dollars on healthy food, clean water, and clean air instead of on vaccines and avoidance tactics. I see governments collaborating with experts on these topics to build new guidelines, govern research funds, and advise the FDA, CDC, AAP, AMA, and other agencies with the goal of restoring health and vibrancy to the population. I see medical buildings nationwide become child wellness centers, delivering all biomedical and therapeutic support.

I see all children on this planet having access to organic fruits and vegetables, to plenty of calories from healthy food, and to clean water. I envision government leaders drop-shipping this food and other resources to at-risk communities and providing plenty of trained and educated teachers, caregivers, and health professionals on the ground to support them and their families. I see the most vulnerable populations—including the houseless, mentally ill, and those who need additional help caring for themselves—receiving healthy food and environmental conditions to support their natural immunity, help dissolve their chronic conditions, and encourage all to thrive.

I see people becoming more compassionate, tired of judging and resisting how other people are. I see people recognizing that we all want the same things in life. I see people finally seeing themselves in others and realizing we are all on the same team, Team Earth.

So, here's to the letting the old ways go. I know it's hard, but it's happening no matter what. You can't control everyone. People will do what they want to do; they will find a way. Let's rejoice in those desires and differences. Mother Earth has spoken, and we must heed her call.

Here is my list of beliefs to consider what is working for you from both the old and the new:

Pre-COVID Paradigm

- ◊ Handwashing, disinfectants, avoiding sick people, and vaccines are the only solutions to preventing illness and bolstering health and well-being.

- ◊ Doctors know more than me. Giving away authority and decision-making to my doctor is being smart. It's being a good parent.

- ◊ Good citizens blindly obey authority. Obeying means you belong to society. Obeying the rules is equated with being safe and smart. How I was raised applies to today's world. Stick to my guns and live the same way is my only solution.

- ◊ I am inadequate at making decisions about my health or my child's health.

- ◊ It's not safe to make decisions outside of status quo. Doctors are responsible for my health and well-being. Doctors owe me.

Post-COVID Paradigm

- ◊ Nutrient-dense fresh food, free from GMOs, chemicals, and pesticides; ventilation and outside time, exercise; and stress reduction are choices everyone has to prevent illness and bolster health and well-being. Living like our grandparents' generation once did restores our health and well-being.

- ◊ Mainstream doctors know their wheelhouse and have their place. There's too much to know and too many variables due to modern living conditions to be one-stop-shopping. They are not nutrition and wellness experts.

- ◊ Question authority and the status quo. Today's world requires taking ownership of your health and well-being. Individualized holistic intervention with natural solutions results in optimal outcomes and reduces the costs to society.

- ◊ I know myself and my child better than anyone. I am smart and capable.

- ◊ It's safe and appropriate to disregard judgement or criticism from others. My health and well-being are more important. Too much is at stake.

I will be finishing my *BeliefWork* companion workbook this year. It will help you map out and organize your healing path, offering insight and choices in a user-friendly format. I believe in you, your Higher Self, and your Source—whatever that looks like for you. You are your own best doctor, therapist, and healer! It just takes focus and practice to be all of who you are.

Resources & Recommended Reading

Here are most of the resources and healing systems I used that I collectively refer to as BeliefWork throughout my book. As a teenager and a new mom with young children I used talk therapy for a period of time.

Energy Medicine Healing Systems

- Accunect (https://www.accunet.com)
- BodyTalk (https://www.bodytalksystem.com/)
- ThetaHealing (https://www.thetahealing.com/
- Tapping (https://www.thetappingsolution.com/)
- BioSet (https://theramedixbioset.com/bioset-system/)
- DNRS (https://retrainingthebrain.com/)
- Reiki (https://www.reiki.org/
- Homeopathy (https://www.homeopathycenter.org/what-is-homeopathy)

- Craniosacral (https://www.upledger.com/therapies/faq.php)
- Family Constellations (https://www.markwolynn.com/mark-wolynn/bert-hellinger/)

Polyvagal Nerve Theory

The etiology behind our physical symptoms comes from our vagus nerve getting stuck in stress mode. Understanding how the body responds is extremely helpful in selecting tools and support unique to the individual. New info reveals that we have not 1, but 3 neural circuits in the autonomic nervous system called the Polyvagal theory:

- Ventral branch of vagus nerve = positive states of relaxation and social engagement
- Spinal sympathetic chain = fight/flight
- Dorsal branch of vagus nerve = slowdown, shutdown, and depressive behavior
- Several facial nerves play a role
- Trapezius and Sternocleidomastoid are key muscles impacted and can trigger symptoms

When we are feeling safe in our environment, our bodies don't have to be ready to do anything. Our nervous system can truly relax and enjoy socializing. We can really connect to ourselves and others. When we feel overwhelmed to the point where we feel there is no point in fighting or running away, we conserve what resources we do have to immobilize. Feelings of helplessness and apathy can result in withdrawal and shutdown.

In other words, our vagus nerve affects our energy fields, which carry our emotions and thoughts. Unwanted emotions and thoughts affect our behavior and our physical well-being.

As I said in Chapter 1, connection to family, friends, and our communities are affected by stress and how we process world events. Those unwanted emotions and thoughts can leave us feeling disconnected and alone.

Consider reading Stanley Rosenberg's book, *Accessing the Healing Power of the Vagus Nerve*. It is a game-changer. We think it's the missing piece to recovery for many people with anxiety, PTSD, autism, and other trauma-related conditions. Stephen Porges is the founder of this new technology. There are many healing programs that revolve around resetting and healing the impaired circuits keeping us in chronic stress mode. The one I can recommend authentically, as I did take myself through the program, is DNRS: Dynamic Neural Retraining System (https://retrainingthebrain.com/). Take the self-assessment questionnaire or view some of the compelling and fascinating YouTube stories.

The law of attraction put me on a criminal case for jury duty this summer. And guess what? The psychologist testifying as an expert witness brought up Polyvagal theory in her testimony! I gave the Universe a high five, confirming that my studies in this area were going to be helpful.

I have used this knowledge to help recover from being triggered. Often, the healing I have needed is to hide out in my room in bed. I've also found that going alone to a public place when I don't want to interact with people is extremely helpful in recalibrating myself back to feeling safe. Sitting at a park watching children play, or walking around a mall, or sitting at a Starbucks is sometimes the remedy I need. The subconscious social information my energy field receives can actually reset my nervous system.

The Tapping Solution

Nick and Jessica Ortner have tipped EFT (Emotional Freedom Technique) into the mainstream. It is a must for anyone, especially teens and children, to consider for staying grounded and tuned into your body and thoughts. It can also clear fears of the unknown and future events. It's a gentle, noninvasive way to reset the body after being triggered.

See these books to learn more about Tapping Techniques:

- *The Tapping Solution* by Nick Ortner
- *The Tapping Solution for Weight Loss and Body Confidence* by Jessica Ortner
- *The Tapping Solution for Teenage Girls* by Christine Wheeler

More Recommended Reading

Books on Thoughts, Emotions, and Beliefs and Their Connections to Chronic Symptoms and Conditions:

- *Change Your Thoughts—Change Your Life* by Dr. Wayne Dyer
- *You Can Heal Your Life* by Louise Hay
- *Ask and It Is Given: Learning to Manifest Your Desires* by Esther & Jerry Hicks
- *You Are the Placebo: Making Your Mind Matter* by Dr. Joe Dispenza
- *Becoming Supernatural* by Dr. Joe Dispenza
- *Shift Happens* by Robert Holden
- *The Judgment Detox* by Gabrielle Bernstein
- *The Map to Abundance* by Boni Lonnsburry
- *Don't Let Anything Dull Your Sparkle* by Doreen Virtue
- *The Work of Byron Katie*

Online Articles on the Science of Beliefs:

- "Girls Believe Boys Are Smarter by Age 6" (https://www.theatlantic.com/science/archive/2017/01/six-year-old-girls-already-have-gendered-beliefs-about-intelligence/514340/)
- "Inheriting Trauma" (https://news.tulane.edu/pr/tulane-psychiatrist-wins-national-award-research-shows-how-trauma-seeps-across-generations)

Online Articles on the Science of Energy Medicine:

- "Gravitational Waves" (https://www.nytimes.com/2016/02/12/science/ligo-gravitational-waves-black-holes-einstein.html?_r=0)
- "The Schumann Resonance" (https://blog.drjoedispenza.com/blog/consciousness/what-does-the-spike-in-the-schumann-resonance-mean)
- "What Your Energy Field Looks Like" (http://innateexperience.net/say-hello-to-your-energy-field/)

Books on the Science of Energy Medicine:

- *The Biology of Belief* by Bruce H. Lipton, PhD
- *The Hidden Messages in Water* by Masaru Emoto
- *The Science and Philosophy of Bodytalk* by John Veltheim
- *Vibrational Medicine* by Richard Gerber, MD
- *Colour Energy* by Inger Naess

Books & Online Articles on the Link Between Trauma and Being an Empath, Psychic:

- *Wisdom, Attachment, and Love in Trauma Therapy* by Susan Pease Bannit

- *The Trauma Toolkit* by Susan Pease Bannit

- "For Parents of Ill Children, a Growing Recognition of PTSD" (https://www.wsj.com/articles/for-parents-of-ill-children-a-growing-recognition-of-ptsd-11550577600)

- University of Tulane Inherited Trauma Studies (https://news.tulane.edu/pr/tulane-psychiatrist-wins-national-award-research-shows-how-trauma-seeps-across-generations)

In Appreciation

To my children that gave me the road map to heal. To my husband who's loved and supported me unconditionally through my spiritual journey. To my adoptive mom who saw the real me at 16 and got me into therapy:) To my adoptive family, biological sister, all of my biological family, and ancestral lineage that demonstrate to me that miracles do happen.

To all of my friends and communities that I've been a part of. To my mom friends peppered all over the country that supported me in creating a new way to live and heal my children. To my bestie for sending me videos, whiteboards and believing in my dreams. To my pretty friend for reading drafts and giving me feedback. To my adult adopted daughter for allowing me to witness vibrancy and abundance in her family and in herself.

To Katy Koontz for validating that my stories and messages needed to be heard and for your game-changing guidance. To Mallory Herrmann for your masterful editing skills.

To my first spiritual teachers Kaimi and Samantha for introducing me to belief work and providing me with a foundation to heal. To the spiritual foundation laid by the masters before us all, especially: Wayne Dyer, Louise Hay, Sonia Choquette, and Abraham Hicks. To the incredible belief work of Bruce Lipton, Joe Dispenza, Vianna Stibal, Nick Ortner, Byron Katie, and Jamie Sams.

To my Reiki and Kundalini communities for raising my vibration and supporting me unconditionally with your love. To my past, present, and future clients and students for your gifts of knowledge, support, and trust.

About the Author

Krista Rosen is an energy healer, intuitive, educator, and author. She's a Certified Karuna Reiki Master and practices multiple energy healing systems. She lives in Portland, Oregon with her husband and little dog. *BeliefWork* is the culmination of healing her family and herself from chronic, debilitating conditions. She has studied spirituality and natural solutions since 2004 and began her journey as a healing arts practitioner in 2012.

She spent most of her life struggling with undiagnosed anxiety, depression, and P.T.S.D. "I didn't even know that how I felt wasn't normal. I just thought I was a weak person that lacked coping skills. I went ahead with the script of life. I earned a college degree, worked in advertising, got married and had children."

Upon discovering that her baby had multiple health conditions, Krista left the corporate world to search for healing solutions. Being faced with this insurmountable task really put her "over the edge." Her anxiety hit the roof and stayed there. She was angry and triggered, which caused her to face old memories about being raised by parents with multiple disorders. She had to face numerous traumas that had been suppressed for years.

Today, she's not only okay, but passionate about sharing what she has learned with you. "I am here to tell you that you can become your own doctor, therapist, and healer. We're all born with this ability. We've forgotten how because our culture teaches us to rely on authority and our intellect while discounting our emotions and intuition."

It is her hope is that *BeliefWork*, with its fourteen personal stories, illuminates a path to freedom for you.

About the Author

Krista Rosen is an energy healer, intuitive, educator, and author. She's a Certified Karuna Reiki Master and practices multiple energy healing systems. She lives in Portland, Oregon with her husband and little dog. *BeliefWork* is the culmination of healing her family and herself from chronic, debilitating conditions. She has studied spirituality and natural solutions since 2004 and began her journey as a healing arts practitioner in 2012.

She spent most of her life struggling with undiagnosed anxiety, depression, and P.T.S.D. "I didn't even know that how I felt wasn't normal. I just thought I was a weak person that lacked coping skills. I went ahead with the script of life. I earned a college degree, worked in advertising, got married and had children."

Upon discovering that her baby had multiple health conditions, Krista left the corporate world to search for healing solutions. Being faced with this insurmountable task really put her "over the edge." Her anxiety hit the roof and stayed there. She was angry and triggered, which caused her to face old memories about being raised by parents with multiple disorders. She had to face numerous traumas that had been suppressed for years.

Today, she's not only okay, but passionate about sharing what she has learned with you. "I am here to tell you that you can become your own doctor, therapist, and healer. We're all born with this ability. We've forgotten how because our culture teaches us to rely on authority and our intellect while discounting our emotions and intuition."

It is her hope is that *BeliefWork*, with its fourteen personal stories, illuminates a path to freedom for you.

In Appreciation

To my children that gave me the road map to heal. To my husband who's loved and supported me unconditionally through my spiritual journey. To my adoptive mom who saw the real me at 16 and got me into therapy:) To my adoptive family, biological sister, all of my biological family, and ancestral lineage that demonstrate to me that miracles do happen.

To all of my friends and communities that I've been a part of. To my mom friends peppered all over the country that supported me in creating a new way to live and heal my children. To my bestie for sending me videos, whiteboards and believing in my dreams. To my pretty friend for reading drafts and giving me feedback. To my adult adopted daughter for allowing me to witness vibrancy and abundance in her family and in herself.

To Katy Koontz for validating that my stories and messages needed to be heard and for your game-changing guidance. To Mallory Herrmann for your masterful editing skills.

To my first spiritual teachers Kaimi and Samantha for introducing me to belief work and providing me with a foundation to heal. To the spiritual foundation laid by the masters before us all, especially: Wayne Dyer, Louise Hay, Sonia Choquette, and Abraham Hicks. To the incredible belief work of Bruce Lipton, Joe Dispenza, Vianna Stibal, Nick Ortner, Byron Katie, and Jamie Sams.

To my Reiki and Kundalini communities for raising my vibration and supporting me unconditionally with your love. To my past, present, and future clients and students for your gifts of knowledge, support, and trust.

Praise for *BeliefWork*

“ This is an incredible read. I've known Krista as a healer and colleague for many years. That I didn't know the extremely traumatic story depicted in this book is a testament to the healing work she has done on herself. *BeliefWork* is a powerful doorway to examine the operating system of our lives and consider if the instructions embedded in our beliefs about ourselves are serving our highest purpose. Krista bravely provides anecdotes from her own life to highlight how she came to have self-limiting beliefs and the new beliefs she created to re-write the code of her life and expand her healing opportunities. Prepare to crack open the book and then not be able to put it down. I read it in one sitting and feel called to come back to it to digest each section more thoughtfully this time. There's a lot of hope and magic in this book.

—Jennifer Boyd, PA, owner of the Boyd Wellness Retreat Center for chronic, complex illness and optimal wellness, Medical Advisor to the Documenting Hope Project, Master's candidate EcoPsychology (2021)

“ *BeliefWork* will draw you in, captivate and enlighten you all along the way. Krista tells a powerful story of her own traumatic childhood, and how she learned that those experiences had shaped a limiting belief system within her. She brings the reader along on her journey of transformation into the gifted and respected healer she is today.

Krista now teaches others how to identify and transform dispensable beliefs into valuable lessons. She teaches us to understand our past, giving us valuable insight on how to identify and clear our own blockages. Her book provides the applicable tools and resources needed to create your own foundation of resiliency as you continue through your own journey of life. Although you may find yourself reading this book from cover to cover in one sitting, it is a reference tool to be used time and time again. Learn to let go of limiting beliefs and build your path to a life of meaning and purpose that we all deserve.

—Theresa Davis, Certified Integrative Nutrition Health Coach (CIHC)

"The events of Krista Rosen's childhood would have been enough to send anyone into a dangerous downward spiral. Yet this remarkable woman somehow survived years of abuse, eventually learning how to fight against her own unhealthy programming and ultimately finding healing and peace. Now, she wants to help others turn their lives around, as well. *BeliefWork* not only tells her remarkable story but also shares the tools she used to change her thinking and transform her life. Even readers who haven't suffered deep trauma will find plenty to identify with here. Rosen's writing is clear and direct, and her raw honesty is a testament to her strength. Her book is bound to help many others on their own healing journeys.

—Katy Koontz, freelance writer, editor for several *New York Times* bestsellers, editor of *Unity Magazine*

"It's not what has happened to you, it's how you rethink those life events and use it to serve your higher purpose. *BeliefWork* changed me from running from the fire to giving me to the tools to put out the fire.

Krista's is the voice I hear when I need to work through what life is or has already dealt me. Her heart to share her life has opened up an objective perspective for me to view mine. Reading *BeliefWork* was transformative on many levels. Memories I had not thought of since childhood surfaced and were healed just by this book sparking the memory up again and provide a perspective that enabled me to put a new truth with it.

I am not perfect, but Krista's book is making me become the person I want to be. Now I am reframing my thoughts and giving myself the tools that I only thought someone with years in the medical field could handle. I have the ability to do the hard work, like Krista shares that she's done to sift through trauma and rename it.

—Courtney Miller, wife and mother of two boys

"Reading *BeliefWork* is like having one of those meaningful, long conversations with a wise, grounded and loving friend. By allowing herself to be vulnerable and open in recounting her own struggles and pain, Krista Rosen offers her readers an empowering hug and a safe place to confront their own personal pain, struggles, challenges, and limiting beliefs. This book is a wonderful resource for anyone on a journey of self-exploration or even those who are just beginning to look deeper into the root causes of any physical, emotional, or psychological symptoms. *BeliefWork* offers the opportunity for a transformational experience for all who read it."

—Beth Lambert, Executive Director of Epidemic Answers, author of *A Compromised Generation*, co-author of *Brain Under Attack*

"I always knew what I believed about the world mattered, but until I read *BeliefWork* by Krista Rosen I had no idea that what I believed about myself shaped my entire universe and how I related to it. Krista shows us how to remove and clear false narratives from our painful past, with examples from her own traumatic childhood. You won't think the same after reading this book!

—K. Jewell

CPSIA information can be obtained
at www.ICGtesting.com
Printed in the USA
BVHW091043240221
600902BV00003B/639